AF263688

DON'T BE A STARVING ARTIST®

HOW TO MAKE MONEY AS AN ARTIST DOING
WHAT YOU LOVE!

GILLIAN PARK

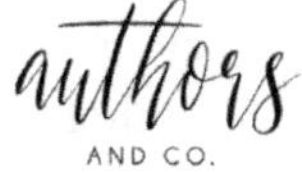

CONTENTS

DEDICATION

This book is dedicated to the unemployable, easily bored, creative, problem-solving, discontent, non-finishing, human rollercoasters we like to call artists.

I hope this book helps you find the answers you've been looking for and inspires you to rise up, create, and make money doing what you love!

INTRODUCTION

We've all heard it … I've heard it for almost 52 years, you've heard it - you've probably SAID it!

"You can't make money from art"

"Art is a hobby"

"You can't paint for a living; you need to get a REAL job"

"An artist only makes money when they're dead"

I'm here to tell you that art IS a real job!

I'm living (and working) proof that you CAN make money from art … but it might not be in the conventional way people often think artists make money.

Imagine being able to chuck in the day job and spend your days doing what you love - and making money from it.

Imagine approaching your art as a business, having the knowledge and skills to create multiple income streams.

Imagine confidently telling someone that you're a professional artist, not just someone who dabbles on weekends.

Imagine your life in technicolour!

I started painting in the autumn of 2010 (just before I hit the big 40) and within six years, I chucked my day job and became a full-time professional artist, earning more than I ever did in the corporate world as a graphic designer.

Plus, I have the freedom to choose WHEN I work, with WHOM I work, HOW I work, WHERE I work and WHAT I charge.

But how?

I got there by looking at other business owners and realising I could apply what *they* were doing well to my art business, and *actually* make money.

I know how it feels as a teenager, desperately wanting to follow a creative path, go to art school, a study in the creative industries at college – only to be met by concerns and objections from teachers, family, friends and peers. I know how it feels to be encouraged to follow a more conventional path, to find a 'real' job, a safe job, a secure job… because it happened to me too.

So, if this is you - if you're looking behind you thinking 'what happened to me? What happened to my dreams to become an artist, to live a creative life?' If you've spent the last 20, 30, 40 years of your life bringing up your family, working in jobs that were… well, just jobs… and now find yourself thinking about what could be, how life would feel if you could make money doing what you love, then this book is for you.

You might want to make some extra money for special holidays or to spend on your family, build that art studio in the garden.

Or you might think you've waited long enough and want to chuck the day job and have the freedom and income to allow you to choose your when, who, how, what and where.

Perhaps you are one of the lucky ones who are already working creatively but not making money (or not enough), supplementing your art with a part-time job. Perhaps you studied art and are now producing work… perhaps you've sold some pieces but what next?? How can you make more money?

Maybe you're an accomplished artist but find yourself on a merry-go-round of exchanging time for money: paint/create - sell, paint/create - sell, paint/create - sell… I'd describe that as a job, even if you ARE doing what you love.

So, what TWO things can change ALL of these situations?

Mindset and Knowledge

Mindset - do not underestimate how this impacts your life, your choices, your determination, your attraction as an artist, and your selling power. I urge you NOT to skip this section, you'll need it!

In the Creative Foundations section of this book, we'll talk about what internal and external influences impact our mindset and how we've been programmed from a young age to think in a certain way. We'll discuss exercises to reprogram and strengthen your mindset, to allow yourself to believe that you CAN make money from art.

Knowledge - and this is the exciting bit - part 3 contains a taster of my signature DON'T BE A STARVING ARTIST® programme! We'll work through finding your niche, your ideal client, growing your audience, selling online and off, multiple income streams, pricing for profit, marketing and branding, adding value and finally, planning your attack.

I confess, my absolute favourite module in the programme is MULTIPLE INCOME STREAMS - it's like a giant Woollies pick 'n' mix of business ideas! Choose as many different 'sweeties' as you like. Not so hungry? Choose just a couple of your favourites to create the income that will satisfy you. And we'll top that up with a final bonus chapter, 50 MORE WAYS TO MAKE MONEY FROM YOUR WORK... but don't cheat, don't skip ahead. Do the foundations and groundwork first to support your 'bag of sweeties'.

In Part 3, you'll find online and offline opportunities to make passive and semi-passive income alongside more traditional selling alternatives.

You'll find information on teaching classes and workshops, selling online on different platforms, how to approach galleries, how to exhibit, selling at fairs, entering exhibitions, creating your own range of products, finding suppliers… plus, creating your values, strengthening your mindset, dealing with missing mojo, and marketing your work.

And if you've gone all icky at the word 'selling', worry not, I've dropped in plenty of tips and tricks to sell your work and your offers without being pushy, forward, or in any way icky. I hate conventional selling. I hate those godawful pushy sales-people - I'd never expect you to do anything I wouldn't.

It's been 12 years now since I started painting as a hobby. In that time, I dabbled and tried things and dabbled some more. I started painting shoes, then typewriters - my mind told me I couldn't paint landscapes - until I became a resi-dent artist at Dumfries House in the Spring of 2014.

In 2011, I painted ONLY shoes - portraits of my shoe collec-tion, many of which were made by the company Irregular Choice. One day, I received an email from Irregular Choice. They had stumbled across my paintings online and loved them… By 2012, I was painting and producing cards for them to sell globally.

I told myself I couldn't make enough money as an artist to give up my day job (I owned my own graphic design business by then) - until 2016, when I took a hard look at the figures, gave myself a goal and took myself and my art more seri-ously. I allowed myself to believe… and then I chucked the day job!

I was asked to teach classes. I said 'No, I'm no teacher' - until I stepped in for someone one day, loved it, and continued to run my classes, making much more money than I had been paid in the first instance! In 2021, I won a Scottish Enterprise Award for Art Educator of the Year, and in 2022, I won two more teaching awards.

In 2019, I toyed with teaching online classes - I thought 'Oh god, I can't go online, I sound/look awful, what will people think?!' When COVID lockdown hit in March 2020, I pivoted the teaching business and took ALL of my classes, workshops and programmes online. I had no idea what tech I needed, but it wasn't as tricky as my mind had me believe. Since then, I've run online groups, memberships, classes, and workshops for over 500 people worldwide. And in September 2021, launched my online Art Academy.

As if that wasn't enough, I've created my own range of products, published workbooks, spoken on stages and mentored other artists who want to create a life making money doing what they love.

And throughout all of this, my paintings and style have evolved. I've exhibited throughout Scotland, I have collectors all over the world and even one in Dumfries House - I like to think it's in King Charles' bedroom but sadly, I can't confirm that.

In essence, this book contains everything I've learnt over the past 12 years, allowing me to live life in colour.

Every day is different, I might be dropping paintings off at a buyer, at a gallery; I might be driving to the coast to gather inspiration for a range of paintings; I might be recording a podcast or filming a demo; I might be teaching online; I might be meeting another artist to help create their dreams; I might be designing a new range of products… I might be spending a whole week in the studio with gorgeous buttery oils, music on, candles on and immersing myself in my artwork, or I might just take a few days off or go for long walks with the dogs. And while I'm doing all of this, I'll be making money from online products, programmes, and classes without me lifting a finger.

Over the past few years, I've worked with absolutely terrified total beginners, right through to experienced professional artists - many of whom have no confidence in making money or in their ability. Oddly enough, it's often the most talented artists who have so little confidence in their abilities and it fills me with joy to be able to work with them, strengthen their mindset, reprogram those limiting beliefs and help them plan and take action to create the business they've never dared imagine.

I've had artists in my coaching groups who have said 'I'm not interested in selling, I don't want the pressure, I just want to enjoy it', but a few weeks later, when that first sale was made - not through "selling", not through knocking on gallery doors, but through being open and having someone believe in them - well, there's not a feeling like it!

Not for the artist and not for me!! I've enjoyed many 'proud mammy' moments, as I like to call them, and look forward to many, many more.

I want this for you.

So, what you'll find in this book is my promise to you - my belief in YOU!

It contains the methods I've used to master my creative mindset, which will help you to treat yourself and believe in yourself as an artist. To believe in your ability to make money as an artist. To believe you can achieve the goals and dreams you've harboured all of your life… and then choose your 'sweeties', the different ways to make money from your work and enjoy creating the life you always dreamt of.

Imagine having a life of true freedom

You wake up in the morning, so excited about your day because every day is different.

You get to paint or create, watching the colours transform your dreams into reality.

You've got the freedom to pop into town for lunch or a coffee, or drive to the coast for inspiration.

On your way home, you pop into your own gallery/gift shop where your creations are on display as framed canvases, colourful cushions, marvellous mugs and thoughtful greetings cards.

At the end of the day, you get to spend your evenings surrounded by the people you love, not a martyr for your art, but a business owner!

You've waited long enough.
You've done it their way. It's time to do it yours.

PART 1

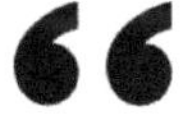

CREATIVITY IS NOT AN INDEPENDENT FORCE SEPARATE FROM YOU; IT IS YOU!

1

____

WHY I WROTE THIS BOOK

As I sit in my studio writing this book, surrounded by easels, paints, shelves filled with art books, piles of sketchbooks, stacks of paintings and canvases, I look out across the surrounding fields, classical music is playing and candles are lit. The candle is part of my Studio Rituals product range which I sell in my gallery. It's the calming 'flavour' and smells glorious … screech … rewind … my OWN range of products in my OWN gallery?!

I've launched an online teaching platform, the Art Academy; King Charles has one of my paintings; I've stood on stage at Old Trafford, talking about the Value of Creativity to an audience of 250 and I've won three awards in the past year! Not even in my wildest dreams growing up could I have imagined I'd be living this life, making money from doing what I love and now writing a book!

It took me 52 years to get here.

In the first 40 of those years, I was encouraged, I was dissuaded, I was convinced, I was unconvinced, I tried to fit in, I tried to conform, I tried office jobs, I tried beige skirts, I worked for Royal Mail every Christmas, I worked in supermarkets, I even worked in Mauchline Creamery! I studied, I chose other paths, I worked in design houses, I worked in publishing companies, I worked in advertising agencies, I worked for Good Housekeeping magazine and the Big Issue, I won design awards, I started my own company, I was bloody good at my job… and I was never completely happy. I was always striving for 'something else. I was discontent and dissatisfied with any achievement because it was never enough. It felt like I was meant for something more.

And in my 40th circle around the sun, I was brave enough to try to build the dream I'd had since I can remember… to become an artist.

I didn't take it seriously, initially. I wouldn't allow myself. What if I was crap? What if everyone just laughed at me? What if this dream I'd harboured since childhood could NEVER happen because I was just shit at it? What if I had never been any good and I'd spent 40 years thinking 'what if?' And then I was a miserable failure? Everyone WOULD laugh at me then! Where would I go from there? So, you can see why I say BRAVE. I don't think of myself as brave but when you choose to ignore your preprogramming, the external influences telling you…

You can't make money as an artist;

Art isn't a real job, it's a hobby;

No one ever makes money from art unless they're dead;

You've heard of the Starving Artist?

Real artists suffer for their art…

Then yes, you ARE brave.

Now chuck into the equation your INTERNAL narrative - those mind monkeys of yours who whisper…

Who do you think you are?

You're not that good;

You can't do this;

You've not got what it takes…

You can see why it might take 40 years of swallowing brave pills to get started, to make those first steps to achieving the life you've always dreamed of… for how long? Your entire life? It's a big risk. It would be so much easier just to ignore those dreams and carry on with the status quo. Indeed, it would be easier to ignore the dreams - creating a life as an artist, and making money doing what you love is NOT going to be easy. You'll be on a high-speed train right out of your comfort zone. You'll feel you must justify why you need to do this to so many people, you'll seek validation which you might not get, and you'll question yourself, your work and your ability.

I can't give you a 100% guarantee that this will work for you but I can share how I became a full-time professional artist from a self-taught painter in just six years, while working full-time in my day job, with kids and responsibilities

And I can give you the tips and tricks that have helped me develop a strong artist mindset, which is THE foundation to your success.

And I can tell you, no matter how hard the struggle has been… it has ALL been worth it!

So that, my friend, is why I'm writing this book.

I'm writing this book for YOU, who has harboured dreams of becoming an artist since the beginning of time but lost them along the way, allowing life, jobs, families, and responsibilities to take over - your time is now.

And I'm writing this book for those of YOU who might be considering choosing art over academia, who are desperately searching for signs that this is the right path, positive role models who have done it already, proof that you CAN make money from art.

And I'm writing this book for YOU, the new graduates, launched into life with some qualifications and no idea how to make money with their talents and skills - this is what they don't teach you in art college.

Start as small and as slowly as you like. Use the information in this book at your own pace, and know that it's always here for you - but commit now to making time for your dreams. You'll find help on how to steal time for your art in Part 3.

Meantime, if you haven't already, hop over to my free DON'T BE A STARVING ARTIST® Facebook group for some support in a fantastic group of artists who are exactly like you!

https://www.facebook.com/groups/dbasa

I want to end with this poem which I absolutely love - Elizabeth Gilbert read this aloud in a podcast and it made the hairs on my arms stand on end. It's written by poet, philosopher and author Mark Nepo. I want to share it with you before you begin this book and as you read, think about YOUR dreams and only your dreams.

Breaking Surface

Let no one keep you from your journey,
no rabbi or priest, no mother
who wants you to dig for treasures
she misplaced, no father
who won't let one life be enough,
no lover who measures their worth
by what you might give up,
no voice that tells you in the night
it can't be done.
Let nothing dissuade you
from seeing what you see
or feeling the winds that make you
want to dance alone
or go where no one
has yet to go.
You are the only explorer.
Your heart, the unreadable compass.
Your soul, the shore of a promise
too great to be ignored.

Mark Nepo

2

NON-BELIEVERS, NAE-SAYERS AND CREATIVITY STIFLERS

We are ALL creative, we're born creative - children are living, breathing proof of this. Just watch a child play, their imagination is off the charts! They'll choose to play with cardboard boxes because it allows them more creativity than their games! That cardboard box offers a myriad of possibilities to that child… but as adults, we see only the cardboard box.

Try this:

List as many uses for that cardboard box that doesn't involve packaging or carrying stuff…

How many did you list? I wonder how many a 6-year-old could list.

Proof that we were once filled with creativity, it was in our DNA, part of us… where did it go over the years? How much creativity is left in the average adult now?

Creativity sources have been depleted to almost the point of extinction. If creativity had four legs, David Attenborough would be banging on about its scarcity every Sunday night on our TV, and rightly so! The human race is to blame for the killing of creativity. It's not intentional but we must become aware of the factors involved in this in order for us to change our behaviours and embrace creativity in everything we do… but that's a whole other book!

We are all programmed by external influences and opinions from the moment we are born. We can, to a certain point, resist the programming but it's coming at you from all angles; it's subliminal, it's repetitive, it comes from greater beings, it comes from previous generations, from the media, from peers, from what's gone before and been accepted, unquestioned, for years. Resistance is futile… or is it?

I have previously thought the non-believers and nay-sayers were mainly to blame for whipping the rug from under our creative feet. They fear what we might do, what we might say. Remove the creativity and we'll all be safe from erratic thoughts and ideas, but I'm not so sure now. The creativity stiflers are a silent and deadly group and I'm going to be bold enough to say we've all stifled at one point, unintentionally maybe, but we have all stifled.

Do you remember when you were young, really young, bringing a painting home? It was just a big colourful splash of paint, a few marks with crayons, but it was created with sheer joy. How proud were your parents, family, carers when you presented your creation? So proud, so much in awe of your artistic talent, it was pinned to the fridge or on the noticeboard.

Fast forward a couple of years, when you're colouring in or painting - how often have we heard stifling comments like these:

"Try to colour inside the lines"

"The grass is green, why have you painted it blue?"

The joy was replaced with concentration and the need to remain within those lines. What happened when you went over the line? How did you feel? I know I wanted to start again because I'd 'done it wrong'!

Creative stifling. How sad that we feel the need to remove the joy to 'do it right'. I've done it myself with my own daughters - I'm not proud, but it's preprogrammed, it's what we're all trained to do!

Fast forward to the teenage years and things are starting to get serious. The choices you make in school impact what grades you get in standard grades, which impact Highers or A' Levels, which impact your college, university or job prospects. I can remember the pain of choosing subjects still and have gone through it twice more with my daughters who were, to be fair, much more straightforward than I was. Mentioning art at this point can often lead to a very different response - a rational discussion about how getting good grades in academic subjects might be a more sensible choice while thinking about your future job prospects. At this point, you're what? Thirteen? THIRTEEN and you're being nailed down to think maturely and sensibly about your job prospects?!!! Sign me up for a bloody pension while you're at it!

The hard fact is, in education, creative subjects are valued less than academic subjects. My education taught me that art is considered to be worth less than academia. Let's take another look at that: art is worth less…

ART IS WORTHLESS.

Now, granted I am a bit touchy about this whole subject. I find it outrageous that certain subjects in schools are considered more worthy than others. For example, the school both of my girls attended was very STEM biased. The harsh fact is that in this goal-driven world, even schools have pupil attainment goals and are pushed to reach government-set standards.

This means by the tender age of 13, we've had our creativity stifled in so many ways and now, when push comes to shove, we learn art is worthless in the 'grown-up world' we are about to enter. Creativity is stealthily removed by education, parents, and teachers - the greatest influences on our young lives and that sounds awful! Why would they do such a thing? It IS awful but not in the way you think. They're not stifling your creativity out of badness, they're stifling your creativity because they ALSO have been pre-programmed to think that art is not a career; no money can be made and therefore you won't be able to support yourself and you will become the stereotypical STARVING ARTIST!

Our carers, parents and teachers are protecting us, they're protecting us because they are fearful, and they are doing their job by KEEPING US SAFE. Fear is the number one reason why they protect us in this way - our mind monkeys work identically, it's a natural survival instinct. They're fearful because there are so few successful artist role models to speak out and educate, fearful that they do not know how to help you, fearful because they want a secure future for you and they've been programmed to believe there is no security in becoming an artist.

Recently, however, the Scottish education system has adopted Art within their STEM structure which has now become STEAM!! Only as I write this book have I been made aware of its existence! I found this paragraph in Glow Scotland, Scotland's online learning resource:

"STEAM removes limitations and replaces them with wonder, critique, inquiry, and innovation"

(EDUCATION CLOSET, 2017).

While I have seen STEM being implemented in schools, I have yet to see evidence of STEAM. At the moment from the research that I have done, it seems that STEAM, while it has taken off in America it has yet to be implemented as such in Scotland. Creativity is what essentially makes us human (Csikszentmihalyi, 2013) and is at the heart of so many things, including careers in fields such as engineering and science. I believe that STEAM is a way to create a whole rounded educational experience that creates successful art integration in our schools and truly enhances STEM subjects. By embracing the arts, teachers can "provide a pallet of learning" and allow STEM to reach new heights." (Education Closet, 2017).

So we can see signs that change is happening. How can we facilitate and accelerate this change in how the business of art is perceived by others?

- RE-programming
- Education
- Successful artist role models
- Read this book?? Cheeky!

HERE'S THE GOOD NEWS

The good news is that the worldwide perception of the value of creativity is changing - dramatically and at a pace! Not only are creative businesses growing in the UK and worldwide but creativity is infiltrating traditional businesses!

The creative industries in the UK have seen a steady growth period through the pandemic, possibly due to small cottage industries being born in lockdown. More and more people are now comfortable with technology, with shopping, buying, and selling online feeling secure.

My own business changed totally in lockdown. In 2021, I recorded the biggest year of my business to that point because my business was entirely run online which opened my audience, allowing me to sell and teach customers as far-flung as Australia. We had a captive audience! It could also be because we had more time on our hands to 'do'. We had time to learn new things, we worried about losing our jobs and perhaps started a sideline business as a safety net, we realised life was short, our mortality became very real - spending what's left doing something you love suddenly became more important. In dark periods throughout history, we turn to creativity to find solutions, answers, and some head space, something to preserve our mental health.

Whatever the reason, the creative industries are one of the fastest growing areas of the economy in the UK.

"The UK had an estimated 2.29m creative industries jobs in the year to September 2021, including 1.62m permanent roles, official statistics show. A further 663,000 creative industry jobs were self-employed."

CREATIVE INDUSTRIES COUNCIL

Creativity previously had no place in the traditional business but as we see more hugely successful entrepreneurs do things differently, and do things creatively, there's no option but to learn from this and be influenced positively. The likes of Steve Jobs and Richard Branson were way ahead of their time. The COVID pandemic also appears to have impacted the speed at which companies are changing the way they work, and the way they problem-solve, because they've been given no option in the pandemic. They've had to find creative ways to make money and survive.

On Wednesday 21st December 2021, City AM News, London's most-read financial and business newspaper, wrote:

Britain's creative industries are essential to the economy, but imagination must shape all our businesses

The UK's creative industries are one of the country's great strengths. According to figures, the cultural and creative industries contributed £115 billion to the economy in 2019, corresponding to 6 per cent of GDP. They account for almost nearly 12 per cent of the UK's international exports.

Creativity is an act of turning imagination into reality, delivery and action. But we must not delegate creativity solely to those sectors. The value of creativity to the UK economy, for people in all businesses and industries, is immeasurable. The degree of creativity in different businesses, however, is extremely variable. While some organisations embrace the power of creativity, other more traditional organisations suppress the imagination of employees.

There are different ways that businesses quash and stifle creativity. From micro-managing to budgeting time and resources, how a company manages their employees defines the level of creativity in a business.

People may feel comfortable with the familiar, but they are aroused by the new.

As we navigate our way out of the trials and tribulations of Covid, creativity will be an even more important attribute. The World Economic Forum has already recognised it as one of the top five skills for the future. Several surveys show that more than half the job descriptions we'll be using in 2030 have yet to be defined. The march of technology will not diminish the importance of creativity but enhance it.

Whether you seek world domination, want to chuck your day job, or would just like to earn some extra money for that studio in the garden, then I hope you find this book helpful and become an active member in this creative uprising of talent, refusing to be swayed by the non-believers, the nay-sayers and the creative stiflers.

You ARE an artist and you CAN make money doing what you love!

3

———————

MY STORY

I'm always interested to hear how someone 'got into art'. I did not take a direct route to 'artist' and creative fulfilment, so I assume every other artist has a similar 'trials and tribulations' backstory. And it's funny because if someone told me they were an accountant, for example, I'd never excitedly ask, 'oh, how did you become an accountant?

Have you always been an accountant?' I'd assume it was a straightforward career decision with no twists and turns. Similarly, if I have to give my occupation to someone taking details in, say, the optician, it's always met with genuine surprise. That person always looks up at me, usually comments 'oh, how lovely' or 'how interesting', but it's always met with surprise. Again, that's not so odd because as we know, our external conditioning has programmed us into thinking that art is not a real job, yak, yak, yak - you're sick of this saying now, I know.

The process of writing this particular section of the book has been both surprising and interesting to me. I'm not a linear thinker and even as I write this book, I need to map my ideas out visually so in each chapter I step up to my giant flip chart sheets, wielding a big marker pen in whatever colour speaks to me at that time and I make a mind map, a brain dump of what might be included in the chapter.

Until now, I'd never seriously considered how or when my art dreams were influenced in childhood. I've never needed to think about where my creative dreams came from or when they began, I've only ever known that they have always been there, for as long as I can remember, that they are strong and at the age of 40, I realised they were an integral part of me which had gone missing for 20-odd years. They became non-negotiable - I'll talk a lot about things being non-negotiable throughout this book.

And so, as I sit here in my painting studio, which has been converted into my writing studio for one week only, I'm almost blown away by what I've found in this writing process about how I have been influenced from a very young age.

THE FORMATIVE YEARS

My earliest art-related memory is still very real in my mind, I've no other memory from this time that is so vivid! I can picture the scene even now and although I'm not sure exactly what age I would have been at the time, I know roughly - somewhere between the age of five (I had started primary school) and seven (we moved from that specific house when I was that age)… let's go with six, a nice, even number, I like even numbers!

Picture the scene: I've come home from school for lunch. It's a fair walk for wee legs. I'm sitting on a stool, legs swinging, at the kitchen table eating cream of tomato soup and bread - honestly, I even remember what I was eating! I can see the TV through the door to the living room and I can hear this strange accent - on screen I see a woman with a really strong loud American accent, dressed in a way I'd never seen anyone dress. Enter Nancy Kominsky.

I know now that it was a New York accent. Nancy had a dark bouffant hairdo and she was wearing a smock-like giant shirt with the collar standing up. At the tender age of six, living in a small mining village in Ayrshire, I'd never seen or heard anything like it! Fascinated, I watched as she stood at an easel wielding a palette knife. By the time I'd finished my soup, she'd created a painting with big bold slabs of colour, barking instructions as she painted. I was mesmerised.

I remember the set being very dark and brown (it was the 1970s - everything was brown), her painting of tomatoes on the vine popped with colour, and I remember a toilet roll hanging on a string below her easel where she'd clean her knife, she had a trolley with a whole row of paint tubes and brushes and she used a palette like a real artist - I was smitten - Nancy did NOT worry about colouring inside the lines!

From that day on, I'd rush to watch her weekly show and I think I probably had no idea until today, as I write this chapter, how much this influenced my creative dreams. This loud brash colourful woman captured my imagination that day and here I am now, sitting in a studio with a whole row of paint tubes and brushes on a trolley. My hair gets bigger by the day and I believe, like Nancy, that everyone can paint with the right guidance and a few tips and tricks. I loved her loud brashness and to those of you who know me, fingers on lips!

Over the years, I tried to find out more about Nancy Kominsky. She seemed to fall off the face of the planet. I discovered the show ran from 1974 to 1978 which fits with my timeline and I learned she filmed those episodes in real time - she really DID make those paintings in 26 minutes!!! I have a few Paint Along with Nancy Kominsky books in my collection and you can find the odd episode online - I urge you to go look. Even now, I'm still mesmerised… and at this very moment, I've had the best idea for a workshop honouring the great NK and her bold brash style of painting for every-one! *Watch this space.*

Around the same time, the legendary Tony Hart hit the screens in Take Hart, an art programme for children. This was a post-school staple for me. The man was simply a genius, a magician with a spray can and a bit of chalk. He made everything he did seem easy, and achievable - it was all smoke and mirrors, creative tricks - and I loved it.

He was gentle and genteel, soft-spoken - the diametric oppo-site of our Nancy. I dreamt of one day owning a tin of spray paint - where did this guy get his gear??? (Again, an early influencer, I sit here today with a large box of various coloured spray paint cans.) But he made art accessible to children, he made it seem easy, and he made me feel like I could do it. He made me believe.

One of my early artistic goals was to have my artwork featured in The Gallery, each week a selection of viewers' artworks was displayed in his gallery, and we perused, searching for our own masterpiece while jaunty music played… I'm humming that very tune now folks, hum with me! Sadly, my first art dream was never realised, none of my artworks ever made it into Tony's Gallery - although I may have stood a better chance had I sent one into the show!

From here on in, my taste for creative knowledge grew and in P4, my teacher, Mrs Imrie (in the 1970s teachers had no first names), would teach an occasional extra special art class. Formulated by her husband who was an amateur artist, she produced drawings of Disney characters on grids. These afternoons were the best of all I can remember in school, it felt easy and natural - although not for some, one girl cried every single time and I could not for the life of me under-stand why she couldn't do it.

Much as I loved art, at no point thus far had there been any recognition of my talent or ability. It was only in P5, during an afternoon of art, I painted a spider plant, which must be the least inspiring plant since time began! I thought it was an ok piece of work but my teacher thought it was fantastic! So fantastic that it merited THE spot on the wall where only special things hang - all of a sudden my classmates became interested, congratulated me and from that day, I became the art expert of the class - that is an honour, I assure you, comparable only to an MBE today.

OIL PAINTS & STATUS QUO

At the tender age of nine, my creative talent is recognised not only by the class, my peers, and the teachers but also by my parents and that Christmas, I awoke to find a real 'grown up' easel and oil paints nestled amongst my baseball boots, Jackie annual and Status Quo 12 Gold Bars record (a double album which I still have in the studio today).

My first **REAL** art materials. I was excited, and nervous and had no idea how to use them! So I set up in my room, opened a book, found a picture of a very green golf course and made a really shit painting. I was gutted, I thought I was pretty decent but this was bad! I remember now how very, very green it was - I'll blame its failure on using pre-mixed green paint, and most likely it was viridian!

But I didn't let it put me off, I'm made of sterner stuff than that. I enlisted in Mauchline Art Club, which took place weekly in the primary school across the road. My pal Janet and I rocked up with our gear, ready to get started, full of enthusiasm and keen to learn from those with more experience… much, much more experience. We were the youngest there by around 40-odd years or more!

One of the group was the previous P4 teacher's husband, MR Imrie - George -the genius who created those grid-based Disney characters - although, unlike his wife, he DID have the first name. But I loved it and loved painting in oils, painting abstracts and tigers walking out of an abstract jungle in very bright colours and this led to my very first exhibition, hosted in the old Mauchline drapery (isn't that a lovely word? Although I confess, Haberdashery is my most favourite).

I entered a turquoise and orange organic abstract (yep, I hear you all), the Tiger tiger painting and a drawing of my Papa's wee dog, Mickey. I don't remember an opening night, if I was there, I'd most probably have been sober but it was such an honour to have my work hang with a respected group and not be treated like a child.

ART SCHOOL, IS IT?

As I moved on to secondary school, I continued to draw and paint continually in my room. I was determined to improve and put the practice in. People forget that no matter what talent you have, it still takes practice. Having a natural ability doesn't mean that's it, you still need to put in the hours. I dabbled with all sorts at this point, mainly drawing, although I did paint a big eagle on the back of my brother's leather biker jacket … unfortunately I used water-based paint, so he couldn't wear it in wet weather, which is a bit of a liability in the west coast of Scotland.

At this point, I never questioned what my career aim was, I just knew I wanted to go to art school. It never entered my head that I would do anything else and much as I was an 'adequate' academic student, I had no real interest in any other subject. I was good at English but didn't enjoy it, I chose Latin to get out of cooking, was bored senseless by history, science was a thing other people should do, geography - wow, is that seriously a subject?? I enjoyed maths and I loved art and modern studies. It was only when it came to subject choice for 'O' grades (Scottish equivalent of 'O' levels), that those unexpected sensible discussions began to happen.

What do you want to do when you leave school?
Me - I want to go to art school, I'm thinking Carlisle

And what kind of job do you think you'll get after that??
Me - Erm, don't know

I don't know anyone else who's gone to art school other than teachers, do you want to be a teacher?
Me - Nope

Then what can you do?
Me - Erm, don't know

It's only junkies and weirdos who go to art school
Silence as I consider which I might be!

I had taken for granted that my next stage was art school. I was naive enough never to have questioned that and naive enough not to have investigated any post-art school career options to back up my case.

My solitary interview with the career advisor didn't help much either, I completed a questionnaire only to be informed that my perfect job would be SHOE DESIGNER - now wouldn't that just be dandy (says the woman with just over 100 pairs) - but remember, I'm living in deepest darkest Ayrshire, in a mining community where a 'good' job is a steady office job, working in the bank or civil service. It is NOT a shoe designer, nor is it an artist!

And so, I half-heartedly embraced secretarial studies and learned to touch type on an actual typewriter with a sheet of paper over my hands so I couldn't see the keys. I cut my nails a bit shorter so I could type faster, just as I did the other day before starting this book. Jeez, I'm finding more and more that this book is a mirror of my early life! And I achieved reasonable grades in a sensible array of subjects which would allow me to get that office job, the fallback, the Plan B.

A massive influence in my life at that time was my art teacher, the late, great Willie Strachan. Again, he was like another Nancy to me - he was tall, he had sort of chiselled features in a Roman kind of way, his hair was a bit longer than acceptable in a 'normal' Ayrshire man, and he was no mere mortal - he didn't walk, he glided through the corridors, he wore green shirts with purple velvet waistcoats, he sang opera in class just because he could. He named my then-boyfriend 'the elusive Mr Park' … he was dramatic, creative, over-the-top, hilarious and above all, encouraging. I'm skipping a bit of the story, but it was Willie who welcomed me back to Auchinleck Academy to put together my portfolio to apply to the Glasgow School of Art.

BEIGE SKIRTS AND TRENCHCOATS

The last years of secondary school played out like this: I was an average student, gaining average results in a generic gaggle of subjects, perfect for a generic office job. I met my now husband at school in an incident involving a purple stiletto - he became the elusive Mr Park - I learned to drive, worked in a supermarket at weekends, made some money, enjoyed some independence, I could go on holidays, days out, nights out… I began to think maybe everyone was right enough. Maybe I could get a 'real' job, enjoy freedom and independence and go to art school later or just paint as a hobby. My mum had a friend in the job centre who would supply endless application forms for decent acceptable jobs. I'd go through the motions, fill them out, go to the interviews and so, at the young age of 17, I gave up my dreams of art school and much to the relief of everyone, made the 'sensible' choice of getting an office job.

I became a personnel assistant for the social work department at Holmston House in Ayr. Before my grown-up life began, my mum took me work clothes shopping - a sensible selection of beige and black skirts, blouses, flat shoes and a trench coat, I kid you not, a trench coat. I was proficient in my job, loved having the money and independence and then one day, just a few months later, I heard the news that two friends had gotten into art school. I remember it clearly, the sun was streaming into the office, it was a Friday, I looked around at my colleagues and I put my head in my hands and I thought 'what the fuck have I done?'. I shared an office with Jean and Muriel who had worked here since they'd left school. They'd climbed the ranks of personnel, they'd spent their lives here and if I didn't do anything about it, that would be me!

I had sold my soul to the devil and given up on my dreams for a regular income, some beige skirts and a few nights out.

Fast track a couple of months: frank conversations took place with my parents - now accepting of my need to go to art school after I'd given the real job a try - and with Willie Strachan, who welcomed me back to Auchinleck Academy in January 1989. I had three months to create my portfolio and apply to Glasgow School of Art – it was the only school I applied to. For me it was the only choice, it was the best and I had to prove my worth now.

GOOD OLD GS OF A

I applied. I got in. And I studied graphic design because I knew I had to get a job at the end of it. It was the hardest four years of my life! I spent all of them trying to be whatever the hell they wanted.

There were surreal moments: sheep videos on walls of parties, designing an instruction manual for a brick, being told in the fourth year that I'm visually dyslexic by a tutor, taking photos of a crematorium as the coffin is coming in, using my pal Crawford as a translator between myself and year hcad, Penny Hudd, who just laughed like a horse!

I had imposter syndrome, and I really struggled at times but all in all, it was an absolutely fantastic experience and an honour to be a student and part of the history of this great institution which is no longer.

As students of Glasgow School of Art, I think we took our creative home for granted, we forgot how important it was in art history, we became complacent about studying in the studios, lecture theatre and libraries, hanging out in the halls designed by one of the greatest artists and architects our country has ever produced. Every nook and cranny was thought about, not just for practical purposes but decorative: every studio door had a different set of 'eyes' set in (they weren't eyes but glass inlays which made me think of the doors watching you as you walked the corridors), the wee window seats looking over the roofs of Glasgow, the Hen Run, which I loved in the rain. When you think of all the great artists who have walked those halls, had the very same struggles as we did, sat on those seats, and were watched over by those eyes, it's a bit mind-blowing.

I graduated with BA (Hons) in Graphic Design in 1993 and promptly started my quest to find the perfect job.

As much as I'm primarily a painter now, I loved designing! If I were to do it all again, I would still study something other than painting because I learned so much in a different industry and I believe had I studied painting, I would have no clue how to start a business and make money from my work in the way I do now. I don't regret studying design, it opened doors to a lot of jobs and opportunities and I still use my design training and experience in advertising, publishing and printing now in different ways.

NO CARRIAGE CLOCK FOR YOU!

If I were to write a paragraph for every job I had, this would be a very long and boring book - suffice to say, I do not employ well. I started my post-graduation career in a publishing company in Leith, Edinburgh. We designed the Big Issue magazine among others. Living in Glasgow at the time, I had to find a way from Queens Park to Leith in the cheapest possible way - and get there by 9 am. It took me a train and two buses to reach St Mary's Workshops in Leith and 2.5 hours each way, every day! I did a lot of sleeping on buses but I loved my work. It was here I learned how to use an Apple Mac - we didn't have computers at art School, they were just coming in when I left - so I was thrown into the deep end and I loved it!

In my third year at GSA, I did an internship at the National Magazine Company in Soho, working on Good House-keeping and Cosmopolitan magazines and I found I enjoyed magazine design, so my first job was perfect - apart from the five-hour commute each day - and then the company went into liquidation three months after I joined! But… I had added excellent Mac skills to my cv and off I went on my quest for work again.

Over the next 11 years, I worked in design houses, adver-tising companies, printers, publishing companies, and repro-graphics. I designed the Scottish Home Show Magazine, worked with the Glasgow Herald, a Christian publishing company, Rangers and Celtic (yes, both), designed whisky labels, packaging, magazines, and books. I became the only female Indigo operator in the UK (one of the first digital printers), training in Maastricht. I learned a lot and each time I jumped ship, I jumped for more money, so I can't complain! My longest job at this point was a whopping 18 months, the shortest was two days!

During this time, I'd married 'the elusive Mr Park', given birth to our first daughter and moved to Ayrshire. Looking back, it was busy! In 2000, I landed my last ever role as an employee, as a studio manager in a contract publishing company in Paisley. I loved it. I had free rein to work as I pleased, the deadlines were mad and the adrenalin junkie in me just thrived on the pressure - right up until I became pregnant again and had sky-high blood pressure. I lied to my health visitor, telling her my job wasn't stressful in the least but she caught me out and I was signed off. I wasn't happy. We moved house again two weeks before I was due to give birth, thankfully our second daughter held off and was born three days before my birthday. I received a phone call from my boss to see how I was feeling… and could I come in for a meeting to restart work, sooner rather than later. Start work? I could hardly walk, never mind go to work!! TMI? He was also delighted to tell me that I'd won a national award for best redesign of the Law Society Journal and that he had collected that on my behalf in London.

That was all it took, a five-minute conversation, to decide that I couldn't be an employee anymore and I chucked my longest job of three years. I am yet to receive my carriage clock!

SOD IT, I'LL JUST DO IT MYSELF

And so this brings me to self-employment. It had to happen sooner or later. Before leaving my last ever job, the deputy MD came to speak to me, he came to tell me I'd never make it as a graphic designer on my own, that I couldn't start my own design business because no one would take me seriously. I don't know about you, but the minute someone tells me I can't do something, it's like a red rag to a bull. Just you bloody watch me! And with social media, I'm sure he did just that!

In 2004, Artroom Design was born and you can tell by the name how I'd begun to think. At this point, I'm 33 and I've not lifted a brush to paint since school! Yes, I drew in art school, and yes, I designed, but there was no actual painting.

I dug out my old sketchbooks and dabbled. I'd draw a bit while the baby slept but it was wholly unsuccessful and I just felt like I had lost any skill or talent I ever had. The pencil was alien to me and put me off doing anymore, I'm not good at being bad at anything, even at the beginning I want to be decent!

My design business grew. I launched a wee magazine supporting female business owners locally, and designed packaging for a lot of food producers and for a souvenir company in Dalbeattie, with whom I had the pleasure of working until I chucked the day job in 2016. It was so varied, I loved working for myself, having the freedom to work with whom I liked, when I liked and on whatever project I liked. I hated chasing money and doing admin but these were minor cons in a long list of pros.

During that time, I also worked on a consultancy basis at Ayr College, teaching graphic design, digital photography and latterly, art and design. I loved working with the students but the red tape involved in doing something as simple as photocopying drove me mad. Working only two days per week, I could cope with it, but being asked to pass a student who had not attended classes, nor completed the work was the final straw and, you guessed it, I ended that contract.

I started painting in 2010. The big ticking time bomb of my 40th birthday loomed large at the end of that year and as I thought back over the previous decade, I realised how fast it had gone. I was swamped with design work, the girls were six and 13, we had now added a pup to the equation and the elusive Mr Park was more elusive than ever, working out of the country much of the time.

What I also realised was that through all of the 13 jobs, the design business, and the lecturing - I still felt like I was 'meant for something else' and knew I had to pick up the brushes and give it a go. I had tried six years before, only to be put off because I was, well, crap for want of a better word. My maturity level had increased clearly and knew if I were to get better, I'd have to work at it.

But how did I fit a hobby into the business, kids, dogs, and life?? Because I made it non-negotiable (there's that word again).

Now, you're reading this book because I'm guessing you'd like to make money from art, or you're looking for motivation to be more creative, so I've decided to timeline my progress from self-taught painter right through to today, to 2022, to allow you a clearer view of what can be achieved and how I did it.

I hope this inspires all of you who have tried to find creative satisfaction where there is none and those of you who think you don't have the time (there's a chapter in Part 3, especially for you).

HOW I CHUCKED THE DAY JOB

SUMMER 2010

Here's the narrative: I'm running a design business full-time, the girls are six and 13, the elusive Mr Park is more elusive than ever before but I'm sitting at my desk thinking…

'I always said I'd paint and I've not lifted a brush since… oooooh… 1989. Right ok, I'm gonna paint, I'm not going to let my being rubbish stop me. But WHAT am I going to paint??'

I look around frantically seeking inspiration and something 'easy' that I will try later that night. Nope, nothing… oh, apart from those gorgeous Irregular Choice shoes I've got piled up in the office because there are too many for my bedroom… hmm, could I? I'd like to, they are pretty damn fabulous.

I start painting my Irregular Choice shoes - very small at first, but they don't fit in a sketchbook so I decided to go bigger. I'm using watercolour and pen on top and I'd call them illustrations rather than paintings but they're improving with practice - I'm fitting practice in between design jobs - paint a layer, let it dry, another bit, let it dry - stops me overworking and stops me worrying about it being rubbish. It's addictive, I'm getting my design work done a bit quicker as I know I can paint between jobs.

By August I start to show friends and family and they were met with approving nods, although WHY am I painting shoes?? Because I love shoes and I want to paint things I love!

My pal Catherine, a florist, is thinking about exhibiting at the Country Living fair in Glasgow in November - if I have some framed, she'll take them with her! Woohoo… that gives me a goal. So, I frame up five paintings in Ikea frames, I have 100 Christmas cards made with a Christmas version of my red IC shoes (It's called Deck the Heels cos I think I'm a wordsmith) and I have 20 mounted prints made of the different shoe paintings.

NOVEMBER 2010

I help Catherine set up her stand at the SECC in Glasgow, ready for the four-day fair. Neither of us has visited the fair, we've no idea what to expect but it's awfully exciting! I paint the end wall red - it's Christmassy and the white frames stand out – I'm well chuffed. I couldn't care less if they sold, I'm just delighted to see them hanging in public (that's NOT strictly true, inside I'm desperate to sell them, as it would validate my ability!). Paintings are priced at an eye-watering £95 and £125 - who the hell do I think I am demanding these prices? I'm a bloody amateur?! (That was my wee mind monkey there)

On day one, two paintings, some prints and a lot of cards have sold!!! I cannot believe it, Catherine is texting me the news - I'm at home as need to get the girls from school and I have the day job. I can't concentrate, this is way more exciting, I wish I was there. Day two - I've decided to wangle a quick run up to SECC, just for an hour. I wear my dress inside out, quite by accident but I think I carried it off well. Another original painting has sold – FFS, what is going on?!!

By Day four ALL of the originals had sold. And most of the prints. And all of the cards. I cannot believe it. My mind monkeys say it's a fluke, I'm trying not to listen.

ONE WEEK LATER

I receive an email from someone who bought a print and some cards at the fair and wondered if I'd like to show my paintings in the coffee shop where she works. Thinks they'd be very popular with the customers there - I google it - Clifton Hall School, a private school just on the outskirts of Edinburgh. Hell, yeah!

I'm up to my neck in December and January as many of my design customers are showing at the Spring Trade fair in January and I have a shed load of work to get done, plus Christmas… oh, and did I mention three out of four of us have birthdays (including the big 40) within a week of Christmas and we're going to Paris for a few days? But I love a deadline and agree to bring work up in the first week of February.

2011

Having received some new additions to my IC shoe collection in the gifting period, I set about painting more - good old Ikea for frames again and I have some greeting cards made this time. Drop off four paintings and the cards to Clifton Hall, and feel very much like the imposter as I drive back home. I arrive home to find an email from Clifton Hall

- they've sold the first original painting already! They hadn't even gotten a chance to hang it!

I smacked my mind monkeys before they could even start their nonsense!

Sales of original paintings, cards, and prints grew through the next few years at Clifton Hall. I had quite a few commissions from people who'd seen my work there.

I continued to paint shoes throughout the year and grow my card range.

TIP: Think laterally about where you sell your work - it's not always in the obvious place.

WINTER 2011

After the success of Catherine's stand in 2010, I decided to find events at which I might take a stand. The very first I tried was Living North in Newcastle. It was a tiny stand and I took only a couple of originals, some cards and prints. It was a lovely show. I was shattered every night I landed back at the hotel. This is where I sold my first 'expensive' painting - I thought I'd never improve on this painting and priced it at a whopping £195… you could have knocked me over with a feather when someone bought it!

I decided to take my first stand at Country Living in Glasgow, at an eye-watering price for 3m of space, but I sold so much that I had to get an emergency frame order and frame new prints each night after the show! Country Living was a massive success for me and was instrumental in growing my audience, finding my ideal customer and gaining a few trade customers in the process. I exhibited here five times here in total over the next few years. I could hear people shout, there's the shoe lady! (This is why it's good to have a NICHE. More on Nailing your Niche in Part 3)

2012

I continued to paint shoes, my customers grew and so did my social media following, so much so, the marketing manager for Irregular Choice found me, got in touch and asked about my work. They began to blog about my shoe paintings and so I offered to produce a range of greeting cards for them to sell. They sold worldwide, with my name plastered all over the back. It was great for the CV but I've never gotten any free shoes, sadly.

2012 also saw my first Trade Fair, which was good for me and secured retailers all over Scotland selling my cards.

And, I don't like to write this but you need to hear the truth, 2012 saw me drift to the dark side - I decided to give acrylics a go, purely because I was too scared to use oils, thinking oil painting was for real artists, not amateurs like me *(bloomin' monkeys)*

I found Hazel Campbell - another positive creative role model in my life - an artist in Castle Douglas who ran weekend workshops. So, I shipped myself off and dabbled in Hazel's world for two lovely days, which changed my work. I started painting florals. They were so popular I had a waiting list at one point. I still do - apologies Shirley Strang!

Over the years, I've returned to Hazel for some much-needed playtime. Each time, it revives me and my work changes just a little again.

2013

I'd had enough of the plastic paint - I needed oils. But first, I needed to learn how to use them so I enrolled in a four-week course at the good old Glasgow School of Art, where Donald Sutherland (not the actor) told me to "Just bloody get on with it, you know how to paint and stop being scared of oils" – so, I just did what I was told and have never looked back.

My next phase was to be my vintage phase: typewriters, phones, and sewing machines. I loved them. lots of people loved them! I still love painting them!

2014

This was THE big year, the turning point in my painting career so far.

In January, I had my first show in a very small gallery in Dunlop. I sold a few pieces but loved realising my dream of a solo exhibition.

In May, I applied to Maclaurin Gallery to be one of the four artists exhibiting there during the open studios for two full weeks. I was accepted. I was delighted and I showed a real mix of work from corsets to typewriters to florals, shoes, and my first attempts at landscapes. It was a fantastic fortnight; the gallery didn't take any commission and the sales were excellent.

It felt real, and I could see my future changing.

In April, Dumfries House offered a residency in their studios for an Ayrshire artist. Along with the application, you had to send in 10 pieces of work and sketchbooks - I was tempted but felt I wasn't ready. The day before the deadline, I had planned to go skiing (no, I don't ski. Don't ask) with my neighbour. I had cleared the diary and we headed to Newmilns to find the ski slope unexpectedly closed… someone was trying to tell me something. So, I came home and used that morning to complete the application, gather the materials and asked my dad to drop me off at DH.

I was speechless when I received a call to offer me a place!

So, straight after two weeks at the Maclaurin, I landed at Dumfries House studios with canvases, paints, and sketchbooks, as the curator, Charlotte Rostek, showed me the studios she casually asked if I'd like two weeks … eh, Hell, yeah!

And those two weeks for me were the turning point in my art career.

Not only did I paint IN the landscape from life for the first time, but I also became much more confident in my status as an artist as I immersed myself in producing work that was selling from my Facebook page before I'd even finished. AND, I'm delighted to say, that one of my favourite paintings at that time is now in the collection at Dumfries House and in the collection of HM King Charles! *(Any chance of a Damehood?)*

The day I left DH, I cried. It had been such a fantastic experience. I could see, even then, the difference it had made to my painting and my outlook as an artist. I returned home to watch the news as the Glasgow School of Art burned (for the first time) and I spent the rest of the day crying about such a great loss!

The confidence I gained in 2014 allowed me to investigate having my own studio - I was still painting in my home office where I also designed and it wasn't easy.

In October, my application to WASPS * for a Harbourside studio in Irvine was accepted and I moved into my first wee studio, up on the roof looking over to Arran. It was perfect. I couldn't believe within four years I was able to have my studio.

Workshop & Artists Studio Provision Scotland Ltd is a registered charity that provides affordable studios to support artists, makers and creative industries

Did that mean I was a real artist?? Monkeys?

2015

By now, I had dropped all of my design work except for a retainer contract with a souvenir company, so two days per week I was designing and three days, I was painting!

People would come to visit the studio and buy, either by appointment or during open weekends.

I was asked by the neighbouring art centre if I'd teach a class - I always refused. I'm not a teacher I said - until one day they asked me to step in as another teacher was ill. I actually enjoyed it and so, I agreed to teach a full-day workshop. Again, I felt surprised it didn't feel like a job. So, I began running classes and workshops here and in my wee studio.

Meantime, I started producing small paintings for Dumfries House to sell, which were flying out the door, so we also introduced cards, calendars, and prints. It became a really easy, steady income.

2016

In early 2016, I had too much work, too much design work, and so many classes and workshops booked - they were so popular that I began running more and more. The regular paintings and products for DH, my paintings, and selling online all grew too much and I knew something had to give.

The day job.

I looked at the figures from the previous year and I could see that I was able to chuck the day job. It was a bittersweet time. I loved working as a designer but I was nervous - what if it didn't work? It was the end of an era but I had managed to achieve in under six years, something I could never have imagined; I became a full-time professional artist.

But that's not the end of the story!

2016 also saw our move to our new home, Lodgebush House, an old farmhouse surrounded by big skies and glorious Ayrshire fields. We converted the old stable into a fantastic studio which allowed me to teach classes and work-shops and so much more.

PROFESSIONAL ARTIST - WHAT NEXT?

I've continued to run classes and workshops in the studio here.

We've converted a room (what used to be an old shed) into a Gallery, complete with oak flooring, gallery lighting and gallery hanging. Lodgebush Gallery opens a few times each year, or by appointment, with a whole new body of work, prints, cards, gifts, art materials, and jewellery by other artisans and craftspeople.

In 2018, I took part in the TV programme Landscape Artist of the Year as a wildcard artist. What a fantastic opportunity and a fantastic day. I was caught on camera cutting my painting in half (it was crap) - and I got to meet the lovely Stephen Mangan. We've been the best of friends to this day!*

*there's only one part of that paragraph that is not strictly true… can you guess which?!

In 2020, as the pandemic hit, I created an online community for artists and I'm delighted to say I have converted so many absolute beginners to the joys of painting and even more delighted to say, most are still with me and still painting.

This was the year I hosted my first coaching mastermind group, teaching other artists how to make money doing what they love and strengthening their style and mindset as artists.

In 2021, I launched my online Art Academy, which hosts a monthly art membership, classes, workshops and coaching programmes.

I opened up 121 coaching for artists who want to fast-track their route to becoming professional artists and have absolutely loved being part of the journey, helping artists build their own creative lives, and making money doing what they love.

And here we are, in 2022. Wow - the biggest year for me so far. This year has been a total whirlwind:

- I travelled to LA with Lisa Johnston as part of her mastermind, Destination Inspiration, to learn from some fantastic global entrepreneurs;
- I had a successful solo exhibition of over 40 abstract paintings;
- I wrote THIS book in six days;
- I launched my signature coaching programme - DON'T BE A STARVING ARTIST® - and I'm now helping a fabulous cohort of artists to make money doing what they love;
- I hosted my first creative retreat in glorious Galloway, collaborating with other creatives;
- I spoke about the Value of Creativity on a stage at Old Trafford, to an audience of 250 at the Bee Inspired event, created by Dani Wallace;
- I sold 29 original paintings in 30 days in July;
- I've had an almost SOLD OUT open weekend, here in my own gallery; hosted some very different and exciting, new, in-person workshops; introduced guest artists to my membership, and won another two awards for teaching!

I've not finished yet!

I'm ending this mega year with the launch of my first book - you have it in your hands, thank you!!!

And by exhibiting my work in the Brick Lane Gallery in London, my very first exhibition south of the border.

I list my story and my achievements not to boast, but to inspire.

I had no successful artist role models as I grew up and believe this is one of the biggest changes we must make in order to encourage creativity and show up for those kids who are desperate to make a life in the creative industry.

Are you ready to rewrite your story and start taking yourself seriously? Turn to PART 2 and let's get started on mastering that artist mindset.

You ARE an artist. You CAN make money doing what you love.

NEVER UNDERESTIMATE YOURSELF.

PART 2

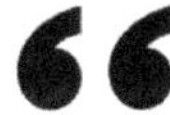

**THE SECRET PATH
TO MAKING A
LIVING AS AN
ARTIST IS THAT
THERE IS NO
SECRET.
ARTISTS FIND
THEIR OWN PATHS
AND EACH PATH IS
UNIQUE.**

ALYSON STANFIELD, 'I'D RATHER BE IN
THE STUDIO'

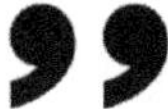

4

MASTERING THE ARTIST'S MINDSET

Artists, creatives, whatever you want to call our collective group, we have creative brains. We are creative geniuses, bursting with ideas - too many ideas for one lifetime *(and aren't they always so bloody good?!)*.

We think differently from everyone else; our minds work differently… Hell, we ARE different to everyone else, we're CREATIVE!

The more I work with artists, the more I see the same traits. The more I see the difference in us and the difference we can make.

We have fabulous ideas and so many of them, we have energy, we are fantastic problem solvers, we are non-linear thinkers, we think laterally and creatively and see things from a different perspective, and we find solutions where no one has found solutions before!

I became self-employed because I thought I was unemploy-able, which is probably true to be fair. But it was also because I have a creative brain, trying to function in traditional roles, in a traditional workplace, with traditional, linear ways of doing things. It was frustrating for me and even more so for my employers, no doubt.

As much as the positives of our creative brains are, well, positive, there are also negatives:

- We're very easily distracted;
- We get bored easily;
- We're not finishers;
- We're prone to overwhelm, self-sabotage, mind monkeys, comparison and that old chestnut: Imposter syndrome ;
- Chuck in Artist's block and I'm surprised we get anything done at all!

So where does an easily bored, creative, problem-solving, energetic, human rollercoaster, non-finisher fit in?

What can we do to rid ourselves of the mental torment of those cranial voices who tell us we're no good, we don't deserve success, we don't have what it takes?

How can we motivate ourselves when there are so many things vying for our attention? And I don't just mean the responsibilities of homes, kids, jobs, friends, family, animals, gardening, and human survival! There's also social media, the internet, TV… Hell, even finding something to watch on Netflix sucks up so much bandwidth!

What tools are there to help us finish just one darned project, help us to just knuckle down and finish the job?

And when you've run out of ideas - and that's the worst - you KNOW you'll never have another good idea again. NEVER! (Or at least that's how it feels.)

Read on. You've come to the right place because YOU are my WHY. You are the reason I created the DON'T BE A STARVING ARTIST® Programme and why I'm writing this book *(with a kitchen timer to stop me from being distracted and to ensure I finish it!)*

5

HOW TO TAME THE MONKEYS

A **Creative Mind - the good, the bad and the downright ugly**

It's all very tempting, especially with our impulsive, creative nature, to dive right into the HOW TO MAKE A SUCCESSFUL CREATIVE BUSINESS section of this book (in the end, I didn't go with that catchy title!) But there is the groundwork to lay, foundations if you will… CREATIVE FOUNDATIONS!

I could go over the old analogy, "you wouldn't build a house before building solid foundations" - you've heard it, you know this already. But the foundations we as creatives need are not physical and we'll need to work on these foundations for the rest of our lives. That sounds very, very long-term and very boring but trust me, it's not boring, it's illuminating and will ensure you're mentally strong enough to build and grow your dream business

"Mentally strong enough Gillian? WTF? I'm an artist, I just want to create, make money and buy art supplies!"

Yep, you are and you do but you're going to come up against the nay-sayers, the doubters, the go-get-a-real-job-why-are-you-bothering-with-this-ers, and that's the least of your worries. Inside that creative brain of yours, the monkeys are at work. They're risk averse, they're scared of new things, they're here to protect you, that is their sole mission in life… aw, those little monkeys trying to keep me safe. Don't be fooled, they're little bastards!! Picture the monkeys in the Wizard of Oz, give them tasers, tear gas and a set of those stick things joined together with a chain and you'll have a clearer picture of your darling monkeys.

They've got low morals and underhand tactics. They'll lure you in with kind words, then boot you in the bollocks when you're least expecting it. You're training your mind to fight these wee tyrants, to recognise who is talking in your head - it's not your beliefs, it's the witch dressed up as Aunt Em!

That was all very dramatic but I enjoyed the Wizard of Oz references - it's my second favourite film in the whole world, so I had to get it in somewhere, thank you for indulging me.

Let's crack on and have a look at the nasties first and how to deal with what they're willing to throw at you, then we'll get on to our strengths and learn how to make our magic sparkle even brighter.

MIND MONKEYS

I've described briefly, in vivid technicolour, how these wee critters work. They're the voice in your head saying:

> *"You're not good enough."*
> *"Who do you think you are?"*
> *"You're not worthy."*
> *"You can't do this."*

The monkeys are here to protect us but the monkeys are scared, the monkeys are risk averse. They hate change so they try to keep you safe by filling your mind with doubts about yourself and your ability. They play underhand games by adding threats of humiliation…

> *"You're going to make a fool of yourself."*
> *"Everyone will laugh at you, you'll make a mockery of yourself."*
> *"You'll come back with your tail between your legs."*

And if the monkeys shout often enough and loud enough, you'll listen, you'll believe them. Remember how we discussed our pre-programming - years and years of external influences telling us that artists must suffer for their work, will never make money, that art is not a real job… your monkeys are backing up all of this narrative from the inside.

We need to do some strength-building work, simple exercises that will allow you to stand up to the monkeys, tell them to shush and get on with building your dream business.

So, how can you silence your monkeys? Firstly, accept that they are a part of YOU, they're there to protect YOU but YOU are in control. It may not feel like it, but you are.

I loved reading Eat, Pray, Love by Elizabeth Gilbert. I had so many lightbulb moments as I read, I felt she knew exactly what goes on in my head! My copy has loads of turned-down corners to reread, but this quote struck me on the first reading of the book:

"Creativity and fear are conjoined twins. What holds people back from being creative is that the fear is so great, that in order to murder the fear, they end up killing off the creativity as well."

And then she goes on to say:

Before I begin any project I actually sit down and have a conversation with the fear, and just say,

---

"Look, we're going on a road trip, me and creativity, and I know you're coming. I just want you to know that you don't get to touch the radio, you don't get to drive, you don't get to hold the map, you don't get to make any decisions and you certainly don't get to touch the steering wheel! But you get to be in the minivan, and I know that you're going to do the thing that you do, which is to just sit in the back seat and scream at the top of your lungs at every corner, at all the horrible things that could go wrong.

> *"And thank you, because I know that's your contribution. But creativity and I are going to make all the choices, and you don't get to make any of them."*

Wow. Now, I've never had that kind of conversation with my monkeys but I'm now aware of when they're playing up and shouting from the back seat of my creative mental minivan like a toddler, and I choose to deal with them similarly... ignore them or distract them, or just carry on doing what I want because I'm the grown up here.

TIP: If a rational discussion with your monkeys is not for you, the exercises in the REWRITE YOUR STORY chapter will help in taming the toddlers in your head. Try each of them out, see what fits, and what works, and there may be a few you can add to your arsenal.

IMPOSTER SYNDROME

The mind monkeys invented Imposter Syndrome and gave it a grand name to inflict yet more fear and paralysis in us.

When you feel like you're not worthy, like you're wearing the cloak of a greater being and it's a bit too big - this is imposter syndrome. You believe that you are not as competent as others perceive you to be, which involves feelings of self-doubt, feeling like a fraud, and feelings of personal incompetence that persist despite your education, experience, and accomplishments.

Imposter Syndrome is likely to strike when you're in a period of growth - perhaps a promotion at work or someone wants to buy your work and you doubt your worth - you're not ready, you're not worthy, assumptions have been made that you are something you're not. It feels fraudulent.

FACT: Imposter syndrome often affects those who are highly capable perfectionists

TIP: Belief in yourself, your abilities and your work can be strengthened in affirmations, in continually building a catalogue of proof and in letting go of perfectionism!

SELF-SABOTAGE

Self-sabotage affects every walk of life, it does not solely belong to artists - in fact, none of the mindset issues we face as artists are specific to our career choice. We can self-sabotage and be unaware of it and we self-sabotage because of fear. Fear of failure - yes, fear of success - yes! Somewhere in your mind, you have a fear of what might happen if you were to fail. What might happen if you were to succeed? It sounds odd to fear success, how might my life change if I were successful? What will happen to the status quo of my life? How will my family and friends react to this new me? So if success is new and we know the monkeys do not enjoy 'new' then our subconscious mind may employ some self-sabotage behaviours to keep us safe.

Here are a few examples in which artists might self-sabotage - do you recognise yourself in any of these?

- Working on a painting for some time and then never finishing or being careless in the last stages and wrecking it;
- Always starting new projects but never finishing;
- Never satisfied with the result, and therefore never really finishing;
- Making it difficult for a customer to buy work;
- Setting your prices way too low or way too high;
- Painting subjects that you know have a very low chance of ever selling;
- Filling an application for an exhibition and missing the deadline;
- Waiting for everything to be perfect before starting something - painting, selling your work, posting on social media - always waiting for the right time (wee tip: there is NO right time).

The last one is my favourite - 'waiting for the perfect time' - I see this time and time again in students. *(BTW there is no perfect time)*

They're not groundbreaking, business-wrecking actions, but they are forms of self-sabotage.

TIP: Self-awareness is the answer to self-sabotage - to watch for your patterns of behaviour and question if you're subconsciously sabotaging your progress. Journalling is one of the best ways to highlight your behavioural patterns and to question why you've chosen to do (or not to do) something which might benefit your business or growth.

ARE YOU A NON-FINISHER?

This comes under the self-sabotage umbrella, by never finishing a project there is safety. You can't sell or use the project, therefore it won't change your business or create any NEW occurrence. But can also be linked to our EASILY DISTRACTED behaviours, it might be that you simply get bored with the project, and you fall out of love.

It's up to you to dig in and investigate the reason for your non-finishing.

I am a serial non-finisher for both reasons: mainly boredom but occasionally self-sabotage. I know this about me and therefore I ask myself why I'm not finishing a project and do something about it. I think of myself as an expert in non-finishing, it's not something I'm proud of but I've become very aware of my foibles and have created a toolkit to trick myself into finishing the job.

Here are my top tips for finishing:

A kitchen timer

This is my absolute favourite control tool! I'm using it right now to write this book - I set the timer for 55 minutes then take a 10 min break. I work flat out in those 55 minutes - I do NOT get distracted, I do NOTHING else other than writing (or whatever I need to finish).

It doesn't work with a phone timer - I continually look at my phone to check how long I have left … then lo and behold I'm down that rabbit hole of emails and social media. Plus, I love the ticking sound of the good old kitchen timer, I find it helps my productivity.

I know, when I twist the dial, I have only a short time to work before my next break - it's as simple as that.

Publicly announcing deadlines

If I have a big job to do - a commission, a series of paintings for a gallery, or a book - I'll announce my deadline on social media to hold me accountable. Normally this is a deadline I've set myself, but the whole of the world wide web is watching to ensure I stick to this deadline. The WWW could not care less if I hit my deadline, but I do because people are watching.

Work in Progress

Again, it's accountability. If I'm working on a painting that needs to be finished, I'll post pictures on social media saying 'almost done, I'll show you pics when finished' - always there will be comments encouraging me to post more WIP and then the final painting.

Your Pile of Guilt

This is a wee extra for you artists!

How many unfinished artworks have you got lying around? I have a pile of guilt - I've gotten bored with them, fallen out of love, got stuck and have no idea how to move it on - they're piled in the corner of my studio, sucking my creative energy. I know I should finish them before starting more but I've no idea how and I've lost interest! So, I'll choose just one, switch on my kitchen timer - allow myself no more than one hour and spend that hour to see if I can move the painting on, change it, rework it. If I can, brilliant, carry on and get that piece finished. If however, by the end of the time nothing has changed, chuck it, gesso it, move it out of the guilt pile.

Bonus - the guilt pile reduces no matter what the conclusion - reward with a cup of coffee and a biscuit!

And onward we march forth to my absolute favourite …

PROCRASTINATION

As a master of procrastination, I can see so many opportunities before me!

This is a bad one, we are all guilty of procrastination and the worst thing is, we know it! I could fill a book with the many, many ways in which we procrastinate, but I won't.

Be aware of this one. You could be losing years to procrastination, I kid you not. It's not just 15 minutes surfing the internet, it's so much more.

Here are just a couple of my favourites:

- **Lack of time -** I don't have time to do xxxx because the kids, the dogs, the budgie, my job, my parents, xxx take up too much time and I've none left to do this thing that I really want to do (fill in the blanks, you've got a whole raft of excuses in there). This is the biggie, the most commonly used excuse by artists for not moving forward and living their dreams. Yes, we're all busy, we all have responsibilities, but I can assure you there's time to be taken if you want it badly enough. Check out the HOW WILL I FIND THE TIME chapter in Part 3.

- **Lack of money** - now this is real, but it's also an excuse and it's genius as you will rarely be challenged on its authenticity! Result! No matter what you're aim is, there will be a way to either raise the money you need (why don't you sell some of that work or teach a beginner's class?) or modify what you're hoping to do and do it on a shoestring. You have a creative mind; you are a fantastic problem solver. Check out the IDEAS section in this chapter for ways to think laterally and creatively.

- **Procrasti-learning** - this is a cracker because you actually DO believe you need to LEARN more, instead of DO more. You can't start your art business, can't go live, can't teach - whatever it might be - until you've learned everything you need to know about still life or oil paint or drawing with your non-dominant hand! Ask yourself why? Why do you need to know everything before beginning? You don't, you're putting off something that's outside your comfort zone and those monkeys are feeding you excuses that don't exist.

- I used to sign up for so many classes and courses to learn more, always unfinished, until I became aware of my behaviour, leading to spending money where I needn't have, and wasting time learning things I didn't need. Now I've gone the opposite way! I'll start something without knowing everything I need, but I'll learn what I need as I go and no more, unless I want to.

- And of course, there are the obvious culprits: the internet, phone, social media, TV… all massive suckers of time and the perfect tools for the professional procrastinator.

TIP: Make a list of how you choose to procrastinate - and watch out for your amber warnings.

ARTIST'S BLOCK

Some say it doesn't exist, some say it's just another form of procrastination or self-sabotage, and others say it's very real and utterly paralysing. I prefer to think of it as 'hitting the wall' or needing to refuel my 'inspiration tank'. Giving it a title elevates its status.

An artist's block (or creative block) is simply a period when an artist or writer cannot access their creativity. Their creativity, ideas and motivation to create dry up. Their creativity or inspiration tank is empty.

An artist's block tends to happen when you are exhausted, mentally or physically. Often it can land unwelcomingly near the end of producing a large body of work for an exhibition for example, or after the work is complete and a sign that a period of rest away from your creative endeavour is needed to revitalise.

However, if you experience artist block in the everyday run of things, there are lots and lots of ways to reinvigorate your creativity! The internet is simply littered with great ideas and exercises to reignite your creative spark.

Here are my favourites:

- Just DO! Sounds simple… it is. Instead of avoiding any hands-on creative work, I encourage you to start working with materials. Start gessoing canvases, stretching paper, throwing in backgrounds on your sketchbook, and anything that gets your hands on your materials.
- Clear your workspace - I loathe a messy studio, but if I'm working for large periods or on a big body of work or near a deadline then it gets into a right mess. It puts me off working, I can't bear to go in. However, if I spend a day with the music on, clearing space, rearranging materials, stacking canvas in size order, or piling sketchbooks on a shelf, it makes me want to start work again.
- Get yourself out and fill up those inspiration tanks at a gallery or an exhibition, or meet an artist friend for coffee.
- Go a drive or walk to the coast, hills, woods - whichever environment allows you to immerse. Take photos, write in a journal, and wander along collecting ephemera for your studio.
- Try a new online class, using a new medium or technique - or watch other artists' demos on YouTube.

- Buy art materials - retail therapy, a delivery of lovely new art kit, happy days.

In my Creative Coaching Programme, I suggest a simple, short visualisation exercise to practice when you feel a slump in your creativity. It takes you just 5 minutes and you can repeat it as often as you need:

Visualisation exercise:

Take 5 minutes out of your day, find yourself a quiet spot where you won't be disturbed, and play some relaxing music, light a candle if you fancy... this is your time to dream and visualise 'what if'.

Visualise yourself in your studio space, surrounded by work, paintings, and sketchbooks.

What are you painting? Choose colours that reinvigorate you. Imagine the feeling of the paint or pastel or pencil as it glides over the surface. You feel part of the piece you're creating, it feels easy, right, it's just flowing from your fingertips. Every piece you create, every canvas or paper your touch is a success.

Enjoy the feeling of abundant creativity... feel the creative glow.

THE GOOD...

We've focussed so far on the negatives of a creative mind, how we must be aware of our weaknesses and how to find ways to manage them. On the other side of the coin, we have such a fantastic set of positive creative traits - let's delve in and find how to make these gems shine even brighter.

IDEA FACTORY

I have no doubt you are an idea factory, a mind like a pinball machine with all those brilliant ideas bombing about, bouncing between your ventricles - a powerhouse of ingenuity!! Ok, I've gone too far, you've got a shed load of great ideas and they don't often dry up.

This is why we are excellent problem solvers, thinking laterally and fashionably out of the box! We find answers and solutions in the weirdest of places, but they work (most of the time). People turn to us when all else has failed, and I know that's because they think we'll come up with a wacky answer but sometimes wacky can work.

The downside to having so many ideas, aside from the fact that our lives aren't long enough to realise all of them, is we find it difficult to switch off. Raise your hand (go on I dare you if you're reading this on the bus) if you wake in the middle of the night - usually a completely obscure time of 4.12 am - with an idea and when you start thinking about this idea at 4.12 am, it grows and becomes lots of ideas, bloody wonderful ideas that will keep you awake till 6.27 am when your alarm is set for 7 am!

Another downside is the shiny object syndrome, yep, another syndrome. You have your raft of lovely ideas but along comes another, even lovelier idea… and it brings its friends - your current idea has lost its sparkle. No longer is it anywhere near as lovely as the new kids on the block! So you lose interest, get distracted and go follow the shiny new idea like the humongous big magpie that you are, leaving those initial lovely ideas UNFINISHED. Can you see how we perpetuate this cycle?

But let's get back to harnessing and capturing all of those lovely ideas, getting them out of your head, keeping them safe and getting a decent night's sleep.

One word: *NOTEBOOK*

Simple as that - keep an idea notebook. I take a separate page for each idea - just get it out. *More on this below.*

You now have a lovely collection of ideas safely stored in a notebook you can refer to forever and if you hit the wall, the perfect place to find a starting prompt.

Another tip: I have a journal by my bed to empty my head before sleep, I often dream about my work, which is fine, but I am convinced this has more or less stopped my 4 am wake-ups.

You're welcome!

OFF TO A FLYING START

With the copious amount of ideas that are bouncing around in our heads, comes our excitement for starting a project. That tingle in your stomach when you know you're onto a good thing - nature's way of telling you YES!

This excitement is what catapults new projects into the stratosphere! I love nothing more than starting a project, a body of work, a new course… a book! It's so exciting. The research, the marketing, identifying our ideal customer, and visualising the sales are all adrenalin-producing.

The thrill of the new will always be a lure for us but before thrusting head-first into another project, which you may or may not finish, here are two ideas to choose between when inspiration strikes - you won't like them but they will save you from yet another unfinished project in your pile of guilt.

- Jot your idea into your idea notebook. Take 5 minutes to work through all of your thoughts and plans and leave it there for now… Let it brew, don't jump into two hours of internet research, don't buy domains, and don't start designing the accompanying workbook. Just let it rest and step away. It'll still be there for you in a week.
- After a suitable length of time - no less than a week - read your notes. Take 30 minutes and write more notes. Do you still have that tummy tingle? If so, when can you fit this work into your schedule? Plan your new project into your workflow.
- Allow time on your new project idea only once you have TOTALLY COMPLETED one of your unfinished projects and then schedule your new project into your workflow.

I did say you weren't going to like them, you don't need to like them, you just need to do them.

ENERGY

Last but not least, energy. When our creative and inspiration tanks are full, we have so much energy and enthusiasm for our ideas, and for our work. I'll often find I'll work for hours then crash, not realising I've been working for so long. Some call it Flow - the creativity is flowing, time passes and you're unaware, absorbed totally in what you're doing. And it's lovely, to be so immersed.

Maintaining that energy is impossible and will be followed with a spell of low energy, not to be confused with artist block. So, finding your sweet spot is how you'll harness your creative energy when you need it most.

When I began to paint in 2010, I was working in a relatively traditional 9-5 way:

Get kids ready and breakfast;

Take kids to school;

Work at desk;

Lunch, walk the dog;

Work at desk;

Get kids from school;

Homework;

Dinner;

Evening routine.

I had followed this structure since I started working in 1993, I was programmed and I didn't question if there was a better way. So when I became a full-time artist in 2016, I was still using this daily structure to work: paint, admin, and marketing. I also felt like I had to paint or teach for the same hours as I would in a conventional job - 9-5. I didn't realise that painting and creating spent different levels of energy than sitting at a desk designing. So much more of 'me' went into painting, so much more thinking, concentrating, questioning, trying to make materials do what I wanted - it all took more energy than I was used to and so my energy was like a roller-coaster and I couldn't quite understand why. People would say 'oh, how lovely to paint all day, it must be so relaxing' - people still do and I have to reply 'only if it's going well!

I started to question how I was working - in the morning I can't paint because my mind is full of ideas and full of what I needed to get done that day, aside from painting. I need to film a class, schedule some social media posts, pack up orders… and I've found through monitoring my energy, that I need to get all of these things done BEFORE I can immerse myself in creating. I can't focus on painting, I become distracted because I know I've not emptied my head, not completed my to-do list. I started testing different times of the day to find when was the optimum time for painting, and when could I enter the flow quickly and do my best work. My sweet spot. I can work at different times of the day now but my sweet spot, more often than not, is 4-6 pm.

I'm going to give you one last piece of homework in this section: keep an energy/flow diary, try working at different times of the day – note in your book how you felt: were you immersed? How did the creativity flow? Were you distracted? Felt it was easy to immerse? After a few weeks, take a look for any patterns, although the chances are you'll already be aware of when your sweet spot might be.

TIP: when you are in a creative slump in energy DO NOT try to create. Do some admin, schedule some social media posts, and take photos of your work. Do not use this time to create, it will do more harm than good.

6

____

YOUR VERSION OF SUCCESS

What does your version of success look like?

We're all different and our ideas of success are all different. In fact, our own ideas of what success looks like will change, sometimes many times!

When I was a child, for example, I wanted to paint - if I could have painted for a job, I'd be happy.

As I grew up, becoming me with but no responsibilities …

My version of success was driven by joy.

When I was in art school, working in the National Magazine company in London, I used to watch the Creative Director and think yeah, that's what I want! My version of success was to run a national magazine, wear quirky trousers and have everyone fear me (she was a tyrant and always wore crazy trousers).

As I thought about building a career…

My version of success was driven by status.

When I was working in a publishing company in the mid-90s, I remember thinking — "ok, when I earn 26k, I'll get a cleaner!" I earned way beyond that but still had no cleaner btw!

As I was time-poor, with financial responsibilities, struggling to juggle a young family and a high-pressure career in a male-orientated, power-driven industry…

My version of success was driven by power and money… and help!

When I became self-employed, it was more important for me to be working with people I liked and with whom I could build relationships.

As I became disillusioned with the 9-5 and opted out of the rat race…

My version of success was driven by freedom of choice.

When I became a full-time professional artist, there was a real combination: I needed to feel the joy, I needed to make money, but most of all, I needed to have freedom of choice.

I wanted the freedom to choose with whom I work, freedom to run whatever classes and workshops I ENJOY, freedom to add different income streams to my business, freedom not to work when I didn't want to, freedom to take time off whenever, freedom to try different things, freedom to paint what I bloody well like without worrying whether anyone liked it or anyone would buy it.

Freedom to create whatever work I enjoy, freedom to create the business I love and freedom to create the income I want.

As I finally had the space to really look at what I want and what's important to me now…

My version of success now is driven by FREEDOM

So, I've come full circle, back to what was important as a child - the joy - while adding the other factors that became important to my version of success since. Now at the grand old age of 51, it's a real combination of everything that has driven me this far.

Your Version of Success will be different because you are YOU and because of what you need right now in your current life stage.

VERSION OF SUCCESS exercise:

Take some time out to think back - what was important in each stage of your life as it changed? Use the space below or a notepad to investigate your various versions of success over the years. How many versions have you had so far? What does it look like right now?

If you're a journalling fan, and we'll talk more about this in the REWRITE YOUR STORY chapter, please feel free to use these as journalling prompts to investigate your levels of success in the different phases of your life so far.

This can help in focusing your VISION of success now.

YOUR VISION OF SUCCESS

I hope you've learned a lot by investigating your previous yardsticks for success. You may have struggled to spotlight that one element which defined success for you at some points, but I hope you stuck it out and got some answers. If you've struggled, check out the journalling section in Part 4, Rewrite your Story. You may want to dig further into your previous measures of success before moving to our next exercise.

You might think that your VISION of success is the same as your VERSION of success. It's not. Your vision is your goal, the dream life you're aiming for. Your version is what you currently accept as success.

We could easily bypass this section and go crack on with the practical dos and don'ts of making money from your art - that would be easy - but this book isn't about making life easy for you, this book is about helping you to achieve YOUR dream of making money doing what you love! So let's just bypass 'easy' and crack on.

In Part 3, we'll look at how to create multiple income streams, how to find your niche, your customers, how to reach them, how to sell to them - how to create YOUR brand of artist. Sound good? And once you've done all that and you're making money, how will you know if you've been successful? How will you measure this success?

Because you will have created your yardstick, your measure of success.

Your aim: your new VERSION of success = your VISION of success

How on earth can I write my vision of success without knowing what can be achieved?

I hear ya! Allow me to help. Remember, this is not set in stone, this is a working vision, you can (and should) revisit this as you grow as an artist. Often when we write our VISION of success, it's easier to start with what we DON'T want! If this is a new venture then sometimes we don't know what we don't know.

Let's break it down into easy questions - just fill in the blanks.

VISION OF SUCCESS exercise 1:

These questions below will help to illuminate what's important to you in your new business, what values will you hold and what will allow you to create your new vision of success.

Write down what you DON'T want in your art business

e.g., I hate technology, I don't want to spend any more time than I need to on a device; I don't want to be stuck in one place; I don't want to be juggling full-time work and my new business

Circle the words which are important to you - feel free to write your own:

FREEDOM

MONEY

TIME

TRAVEL

MY OWN SPACE

RECOGNITION

PEOPLE

STATUS

REPUTATION

JOY

FUN

HUMOUR

SECURITY

ADVENTURE

RISK

POWER

FLEXIBILITY

CONTROL

INTEGRITY

ATTAINABLE

ELITE

APPROACHABLE

VALUE

ABUNDANCE

BOLD

Now craft your vision of success - there's no need to be specific about how you'll achieve this vision, there's no need to list what products or offers you'll sell, we'll get to that later.

E.g. (Using your DON'T want list and the words, FREE-DOM, TRAVEL, SECURITY, JOY)

I love to travel and enjoy creating wherever and whatever I please. I am growing a business which allows me this freedom, providing me with enough income to afford the security, allowing me to reduce my day job by XX (or chuck it completely).

VISION OF SUCCESS exercise 2:

Now complete this sentence - try to find the **ONE key** value in your VISION statement

My vision of success is driven by …

Write your exercise 1 VISION OF SUCCESS somewhere you can see it regularly and keep this in mind as we move on to rewriting your story.

7

REWRITE YOUR STORY - REPROGRAMMING

DON'T BE A STARVING ARTIST® programme is mainly a practical business course designed specifically to show artists how to make money from their work.

It contains twelve modules and out of those, ten are practical 'how to' classes on how to find your niche, your ideal client, growing your audience, selling, multiple income streams, pricing for profit, marketing & branding, creating the experience, and planning. Implement these modules and you'll have a business which you can grow to whatever level you like, but without completing the first two modules, many artists will struggle.

Mastering the Artist Mindset - THE most important modules in this programme. I call these modules my Creative Foundations.

At the beginning of the book we discussed how we've been pre-programmed from birth by society, parents, teachers, peers, education, media - external influences. As much as we don't want to believe this pre-programming, we really have no choice in the matter.

So, before we make a start into the practical nitty-gritty of crafting your dream of making money as an artist, we need to take the time to reprogramme. So far, we've learned about those nasty little critters living in your head, about our creative habits - good and bad, we've created a vision of our success and I'd like you to have that visible as we go through these strengthening exercises and rewriting your story.

PRE-PROGRAMMING VS RE-PROGRAMMING

We've looked at the reasons why we've been programmed to think automatically of the Starving Artist stereotype and to doubt the viability of making money as a creative business but we must make our head roads (pardon the pun) into resetting and reprogramming how we think as this will allow us to build our defence system and master the artist mindset.

Once you've looked back at the narrative of your early years, it's time to rewrite it as we go forward. This will take some time and persistence, continuing to use whichever methods work best for you whenever you feel your resistance slipping or beginning to doubt yourself as an artist and in following your creative path.

In module one of the DON'T BE A STARVING ARTIST® live programme, we delve much deeper into your past experiences and how your perception of art and creativity was carved but that's a whole other book… and now an online programme… so for now, let's have a look at some exercises to strengthen your mindset as an ARTIST.

These are not one-time-only exercises - if you dream of having a six-pack, you wouldn't do sit-ups for one day then wait for your six-pack to arrive!

It's the same with mindset, it takes work and perseverance and it's very easy just to give up. I do not want this for you! I want to make the mindset work fun, not a chore.

RE-PROGRAMMING EXERCISES:

PRINTED PROOF

Keep ALL positive responses to your artwork.

Social media is fantastic for this but it's great to have so many positives in one place. Take screenshots and photos, or copy & paste ALL positive comments, print them out, chop them up into separate comments and keep them in a jar or a book so you can look at them regularly in all their full glory.

When you're doubting yourself and this new life you want to create, get your jar out, and read those comments IN HARD PRINT. Just five minutes of reading this positive feedback can get you back on track.

JOURNALLING

Journalling is my favourite!!!

I try to make time to journal regularly but when I first started, I was not convinced: What do I write? What's the point if no one sees it? I feel bloomin' daft! These are all normal reactions.

However, I've had the best ideas for paintings and workshops while I journaled and I now even have a bedside journal because I dream about my work a lot and this is my way of getting things out of my head before sleep. I still dream about work but it's definitely less so now. My bedside journal also allows my subconscious to work on any confusion or questions I might have as I sleep - stops me from waking at 4 am, trying (and failing) to find solutions.

Give it a try - it is a fantastic way to deal with those mind monkeys we have in our heads.

Not sure what to write? I'll pop three prompts in the REWRITE section to get started, I recommend starting with a question, and then simply allow the pen to flow with any answers and thoughts.

And please DO use a pen and paper. Writing by hand connects you with the words and allows your brain to focus on them, understand them and learn from them.

AFFIRMATIONS

This is love or hate. Repeating positive words over and over to yourself has been proven to have a strong effect on how you think - used by many athletes to psych up for big games etc. My advice? Write your affirmations in the way you would speak. Don't just copy and paste from the internet - it needs to sound like you.

Practice your affirmations a few times each day - some recommend in front of a mirror, you may feel icky. Just do what feels right.

If saying affirmations out loud is not for you, then try writing the affirmations and pinning them where you can see them regularly.

PEER SUPPORT

I cannot over-emphasise the importance of surrounding yourself with people who understand what you're going through, and who can appreciate the ups and downs as you grow as an artist, creating your business. Being an artist can be a lonely place, you may find that very few of your family and friends will understand why this is so important to you and find it difficult to discuss with them.

Find your tribe - online, offline or both! Is it a weekly art group, or online art community? This is the perfect time to pop a link here for my free DON'T BE A STARVING ARTIST® Facebook group: https:// www.facebook.com/groups/dbasa, where you'll find lots of creatives just like you.

VISION BOARD

Gather your dreams: art you'd love to make, galleries you'd love to visit or exhibit in, the new kitchen you'd love, holidays you'll take, your dream studio…

Get them all on there. This is your WHY. Keep your vision board in sight - if you have a studio space, this is the perfect spot and when the going gets tough, remember the WHY.

TIP: I like to use a pinboard. As my vision changes, I can move it around and add to it without recreating a whole new board.

REWRITE YOUR SCRIPT

This is so powerful and it might take a few attempts (it'll probably also change like your Vision Board). I did this about 10 years ago and I still have my rewritten script - I've gone way beyond what I wrote then but I remember at the time thinking, 'if only', not quite trusting the process but willing to take a chance.

Write your dream 'Day in the Life'… 'Week in the Life'…

REWRITE YOUR SCRIPT EXERCISE 1:

But first of all, I'd like you to ask yourself three questions because oddly enough, we struggle to call ourselves an ARTIST **these are perfect journal prompts**

Can you call yourself an artist? If not - why not?

What holds you back from this?

What has to happen for you to class yourself as an artist?

REWRITE YOUR SCRIPT EXERCISE 2:

Now - allow yourself to be that ARTIST.

Find a quiet spot where you won't be interrupted, pour yourself a lovely hot drink or glass of wine, light a favourite candle and grab a pen and a notepad (if you're like me and every other creative I know, you'll have shed loads of gorgeous stationery you can't resist buying!)

Take an hour or two on your own, settle in and enjoy dreaming about how life might be. What success might look like for you?

Think about yourself living the life of an artist.

How much or how little time is spent on your art business?

Are you delivering paintings to a local gallery?

Immersing yourself in a new body of work and playing with gorgeous materials?

Taking a road trip for some inspiration?

Painting en Plein air by the sea, while slurping from a flask of hot coffee?

Meeting friends for lunch or thrashing out new ideas?

Visiting an exhibition?

Meeting with a gallery about your forthcoming exhibition?

Planning kids after school class?

Taking an art retreat somewhere sunny?

Delivery of your new products has arrived and you're taking pics for social media cos you're so excited about how bloody fantastic they look?

Are you teaching a small group of new artists?

Are you filming a demo online?

How much time are you enjoying with family and friends - and while you're doing that, are you making money from online sales with no input from you?

Are you taking a camper van through France, filling sketchbooks, painting as you stop in those quaint villages, by fields of sunflowers and lavender? I might just have added one of my own there.

These are your dreams - write about your ideal day/weekend/week in the life of an artist.

FINALLY - TAKE YOURSELF SERIOUSLY

If you don't, who will?

Why can't we call ourselves ARTISTS? Why do we need someone else's validation to become an ARTIST? Wee head's up… you don't. So let's start now.

If you were a checkout operator and someone asked what you do, you'd tell them 'Checkout operator', no qualms, you wouldn't feel odd or unworthy. You wouldn't need to quantify your job description. So, find your word - is it ARTIST? Is it CREATIVE? Is it PAINTER? You choose. Get comfortable with it and don't shy away from the label.

WARNING:

When I chucked the day job in 2016, I struggled with the label (I didn't have the creative foundation mindset work or DON'T BE A STARVING ARTIST® programme to guide my way) - if someone asked, I'd say I was a 'painter' - they automatically assumed a painter and decorator! They'd usually launch into their decorating dreams, issues with finding reliable painters, blah, blah, blah… I had to wait

patiently to say 'no, I mean I'm a painter, like an artist'…
LIKE AN ARTIST?! Not just 'an artist'?!

So don't waste time listening to folk's decorating woes -
own it!

YOU ARE AN ARTIST

and you CAN make money doing what you love!

PART 3

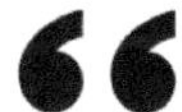

MAKING
MONEY IS ART
AND WORKING
IS ART AND
GOOD
BUSINESS IS
THE BEST ART

ANDY WARHOL

8

WELCOME TO DON'T BE A STARVING ARTIST®

THE BITE-SIZE VERSION

You've made it!

Now you've fully set your intentions as an artist, let's get stuck into the ways you can make money from your work and the practical aspects of creating your business.

Part 3 is a bite-size version of my signature DON'T BE A STARVING ARTIST® programme, which is available as an online DIY course or delivered live annually.

In this section, we'll take a look at whether you're ready to start a business, but don't worry, there are tips in the first chapter to help you progress to a stage of readiness.

Time is a big issue for all of us, we all live busy lives, so firstly, let's take a look at how to create the time you'll need.

Moving into nailing your niche and finding your ideal customer - don't skip these sections, honestly, these are so important to grow your business more quickly, wasting less time and money!

My absolute favourite - the big Woolies Pick 'n' Mix of Business Ideas - multiple income streams to everyone else. Yum, I want to do ALL of them, or have done them at some point.

Pricing and selling are two subjects I'm most asked about, I've tried to answer all of the questions before you need to ask them in these chapters.

Finally, marketing and branding - these sound so grand, but they're just about common sense and consistency. You'll find a few guidelines here on how to create YOUR brand of artist.

And as a treat, especially for you, I've added a BONUS CHAPTER - 50 MORE Ways to Make Money as an Artist. I don't want you to run out of ideas for that notebook of yours.

Off you go and enjoy!

Are You Ready For This?

At every new stage as we grow as an artist - in fact, in every new stage of life - we'll question if it's right, if we're ready. It's only natural to question whether we're ready for that next stage if we have what we need to achieve and be successful at that next level.

In 1989, I questioned if I was good enough for the Glasgow School of Art.

In 1994, I questioned if I were ready to run the studio of a publishing company.

In 2004, I questioned if I could start my own design company after being employed.

In 2010, I questioned if I were brave enough to start painting - what if I was crap and my lifelong dream went up in smoke?

In 2016, I questioned if I could make it as a full-time artist and chuck the day job.

In 2022, I questioned if I was ready for a high-end mastermind.

In 2022, I questioned if anyone would sign up to my signature programme.

In 2022, I questioned if I could get on a stage in front of an audience of 250.

In 2022, I questioned if my work was good enough for a London gallery.

In 2022, I questioned if I could write a book.

And I can see a pattern here - I'll continue to question every next stage of development and rightly so. Notice that I am questioning MORE, not less, as I grow as an artist and in business! NOT questioning if we qualify for the next level is probably a sign of a psychopath, or certainly a massive ego!

There are usually some signs if you're open to seeing them, but I have good news, you don't need to look too hard to know you're ready to start making money from your work.

Here are five sure signs that you're ready:

SIGN 1 - people WANT your work!

A mahoosive clue is when friends and family start asking for your artwork or dropping heavy hints that they'd love to own some of your work. They might even ask if you'll paint their favourite place or their pet, or send you photos saying you might like to use them for your work.

You may be giving your paintings to friends for gifts - you may be convincing yourself, they're only taking them because they're free. Please remember, no one hangs something they hate on their wall! If someone hangs your painting in their home, they hang it because they LIKE IT!

If you're a secret artist and no one has seen your work, then embrace social media. You need to know what your audience likes. Popping your work onto your personal profiles will give you the feedback you need. Yes, it's scary, you're laying your soul on the line (online, even) - what if no one likes it, it's like a personal rejection… but please give it a try. I can almost guarantee the response to your work will boost your confidence, not batter it.

Post some pics of your artwork on your social media platforms. Facebook, Instagram, and Pinterest are all visual platforms. The willing public will soon let you know what they think.

You don't need a business page at this stage - you just want to post on your personal page.

Ask questions, and engage with your audience because even if they are only your aunts, cousins and hairdresser, they could very well be your customers and they do have an opinion, which is all you want at this stage.

TIP: Remember to make your page PUBLIC, not private. The more engagement you can get, the better. And you never know who might be the friend of your friends, they could be your next customer.

SIGN 2 - Do YOU like what you see?

Many emerging artists overlook this. Would YOU be happy to see your work hanging on a friend's wall, an exhibition, a gallery, local shop?

Granted that's an odd question but if you're producing work that YOU DON'T like, you won't sell it - no matter how good it is. Your personal feelings will come across every time you talk about it. We won't like every piece we produce but we need to be happy with the majority of our work.

No one wants to buy from an artist who doesn't value their work. People buy from people and your customer wants to know you have a real passion and love for your creativity, your practice and your art.

TIP: You may be in the early stages of your artistic journey and not sure what fits quite yet. Keep putting in the hours of practice - don't judge your output - experiment and play until you find what you love doing. Only then will you begin to love what you produce.

SIGN 3 - Do you have your own STYLE?

Are you producing original art or just replicating what teachers, tutors and other artists teach in classes, tutorials and workshops?

If you are producing artwork from your own reference materials and are confident in working with your chosen mediums, then you're good to go.

Don't overanalyse having a 'style' - people don't realise they have a style but EVERY independent choice and decision YOU make as you create: the materials you use, the subjects you choose, the format, composition - these are all part of YOUR STYLE.

TIP: If you are still reproducing paintings from step-by-step tutorials by other artists, then you are not ready. You need to start producing work from your own references - whether that's from sketches you've produced or photos you've taken.

I prescribe the same 'next steps' as No. 2: Keep putting in the hours of practice - don't judge your output - experiment and play until you find your voice.

Think about every choice you make. Find the subjects you love to paint, what colours you prefer, what materials you love working with, and what formats and compositions you favour.

I'm a big advocate of painting only what you love, using only the materials you love… this will help hone your creative signature style.

SIGN 4 - Are you taking your art seriously by investing in decent-quality materials?

You've tried the cheap-as-chips canvases in the supermarket, you've tried the multi-packs of student paint, you're fed up with the poor-quality output and now invest in quality materials, which you love to use… cos (as Jennifer would say) you're worth it.

There are many ways to make money from art but if you want to sell your original pieces, then they need to be created using quality materials. If you made your best painting using poor quality materials - because you thought you were just messing about - how sick would you be?

Always use the best materials you can afford. You'll love using them more and your love will show in the finished piece.

TIP: If you're on a budget there's no need to spend a fortune on ALL new materials, ask artist friends for recommendations on one or two products to start with (Facebook I find is fantastic for this).

If you're a painter, I would recommend in upgrading the surface you work on first, most known-brand student quality paints are pretty decent but if you're working on a substandard canvas or use cheap, nasty watercolour paper, eurgh, it's a rough ride.

Build up your supplies gradually - make a wish list to dish out at birthdays and Christmas - or ask for vouchers from your favourite art store. Watch out for online sales and deals and sign up to your favourite online art shop for discounts.

SIGN 5: Two Ps... Passion and Prolific

Oh Lordy, this is my favourite soapbox subject - PASSION! It's the biggie for me. You'll need passion in spades!

Your passion will show in your paintings and in the way you communicate. It will shine from you when you talk about your art and your process… it will also keep you going to be PROLIFIC!

People think an artist just sits around waiting on the arrival of their muse, waiting until inspiration strikes… now wouldn't that just be lovely?!

Sadly, that is NOT the case. A working artist needs to be prolific, they need to put the work in.

They need to keep showing up. Get into that studio and just put the hours in - it's as simple as that.

Your passion for what you do will keep you going when you lose motivation, hit the wall and when the next big P strikes - Procrastination.

If you have paintings stashed everywhere, if your family moan constantly about the dining room table being covered in your 'stuff' (or often referred to as another word beginning with S) if you're giving paintings to friends and family to make space… the passion is there and you, my darling, are READY TO SELL!

TIP: Not quite there yet? Here it comes again… experiment, play, create, paint… if you struggle to find the time, then make a non-negotiable schedule.

Block that time out each day or each week to put the work in and remember (more P's): **Progress over Perfection!**

Don't overanalyse, don't throw things in the bin on a bad day, just keep producing until you begin to know it's right, it's there, it's finished - because you'll know when it's working and so will everyone else.

So, are YOU ready to sell?

If you can say YES to at least three of these Signs, then I can be fairly certain that you're ready to make money from your art.

Remember, an artist can make money in many, many ways other than selling original artwork - I've made 10 and 20 times the original selling price of an artwork from spin-off products and offers.

No longer do we make money ONLY from galleries selling our paintings. You don't need to sell through galleries at all if it's not for you.

Multiple income streams and recurring revenue will ensure you will not be that Starving Artist and allow you to take control of your creative career.

Everything else you need can be learned: presentation, selling, tech, pricing, creating saleable products, making prints, shipping, finding customers, keeping customers, marketing, and admin.

What you can't learn is the passion inside of you which will drive your dreams into reality.

So, if you have that passion, read on. Let's start making money!

9

___

WHERE WILL I FIND THE TIME

'Aw, it's ok for you Gillian, you know what you're doing. I've no idea, I've no time, I'm working, I've got the kids…'

I've heard it all before, hell, I've used it myself!

We use time as the biggest procrastinator but it's simply an excuse. An excuse to ourselves and to anyone willing to listen. It justifies why you can't make those dreams a reality. It's a protector of your fear. It's EASY!

Yes, of course, you're busy, we all are. But we all have the choice in how we SPEND our time and that's how we have to look at it. We have to BUDGET wisely. We have to look at our time and decide where to spend it, and what gives us the most value.

If you take a serious look at how you spend your time, and I mean serious, take note of everything you do for a week. How long do you spend mindlessly surfing, scrolling through Facebook, watching TV, rummaging through eBay, or trying to find something to watch on Netflix?

My downfall is trawling mindlessly through social media - it's so very easy to fall down that rabbit hole and lose an hour or three.

Life would be so easy if we could rely on our willpower to stop us from this mindless time spent but I know no one who has that level of self-control. We need to find a trick that'll do the job for us.

Firstly, take a long hard look if you're using time as your excuse NOT to take active steps in living your dreams.

When I began painting in 2010, I was running my own design business full-time, my husband worked overseas approximately 40% of the time, and my daughters were six and 13 and needed all the taxiing to various groups, clubs, and friends as they do at that age. We had a caravan in Lendalfoot which we visited most weekends, we had just moved home and I decided we should add a pup to this whole shebang.

There was very little me-time left but I remembered my dream of becoming an artist and I realised time was flashing past at an awful pace. I was nearly forty and still restless with the notion that I was here for 'something else'. I knew I wanted to be a painter but I hadn't painted since school - I was shit scared that I couldn't do it! I was shit scared that I'd be shit! But I owed it to myself to try - to make time for the only career dream I'd ever had since I first painted that spider plant in P5!

So, I made it my business to find an hour here and there, and the more time I spent, the more I enjoyed it, the more I realised 'this was it' and the more I was prepared to sacrifice to realise my creative dreams.

It became non-negotiable.

It's amazing what you can achieve when you want something badly enough.

So, that's how I got started - tiny chunks of time, learning how to paint, making mistakes, making bloody awful paintings, getting better, finding what I loved, finding what worked for me - finding the joy, finding the confidence.

Are you prepared to sacrifice an hour of scrolling to find love?

I can't answer that question, that's for you to decide.

So, back to the practicalities of finding the time:

Where can you carve some time?

Where will you create?

What do you need to learn?

Who can you learn from?

Where can you find support?

Where can you show your progress?

Answer these questions first then go grab yourself a diary or calendar or planner and block off YOUR creative time, making it non-negotiable… then SHOW UP and do the work, whether you feel like it or not. Lack of time is NOT your excuse anymore.

Time blocking

Our creative minds are like feral animals needing to be reined in! Don't allow that animal to mess with your creative schedule.

Even now, maybe even more so, my mind is like a feral animal, I still need to trick myself into doing things, even things I enjoy (that's the madness of the creative mind).

Time blocking is your friend - time blocking holds you accountable. I have a new best friend in my time-blocking arsenal - I'm using it right now to write this book - a £4 kitchen timer. Honestly, the best £4 I've spent in a very, very long while.

I tried setting timers on my phone - and when I hit a rough patch in a painting or just got bored or distracted - I'd go check my phone to see how long I had left in that time block. Do you know what happened next? Yep, Facebook or Instagram or email started batting their eyelashes at me - look at me Gillian, you know you want to! Next thing I know, I've lost an hour, bought two new pairs of Moda en Pelle shoes, three upcycling books, a set of drumsticks, searched for piano lessons locally and now have no intention of getting back to work. **the listed items are a real live online rabbit hole session**

Now I leave my phone in another room and use my kitchen timer. I don't set it for any longer than 55 minutes because we creative minds get very bored and restless after that.

Try it. You'll be amazed at how much you get done in that time - and then give yourself a little treat at the end of it, take a 10 minutes break and do it all again.

I wish someone had given me this advice in 2010… or at least before 2022!!

10

MAKE LIKE MARMITE - NAIL YOUR NICHE

I teach many different styles, different techniques and mediums, and different subjects, I encourage experimentation, playing and trying new things which are vital to your growth as an artist. However, nailing your niche is one of the most important things you can do for yourself as a successful artist!

I WANT people to dislike your work!

You want to be like Marmite - love or hate. The grey land of indifference is of no use to an artist. No one has ever bought a painting because they felt indifferent to it! Few people (especially as money gets tight) buy paintings because they are just 'nice'. They can go to Next for their matchy-matchy prints and homewares - you are here to produce work that you are passionate about, we, as artists, have no interest in indifference!

Controversial, I hear you say. It's been said many times to my face!

> *"I don't want to just do one thing forever."*
> *"But won't that restrict buyers? I'd rather appeal to more people, than less."*
> *"That doesn't make business sense to restrict my art to a small group."*
> *"But I love trying new things and would get bored doing the one thing over and over."*

I've heard it all.

Let me explain my WHY ...

Establishing your niche allows you to focus on one specific area - a style, a type of work, a subject - and by doing that you can find your IDEAL CUSTOMER more easily and speak to them personally.

I don't mean you're gonna ring them up for a chat, I mean through all of your communication, all of your marketing, all of your messaging - you're going to speak to just that ONE PERSON. You'll use their language, the words and phrases they use and they're going to know you're speaking directly to them, offering them something they really, really want and will hopefully buy.

For example, if you paint dogs, you can reach your ideal buyers at dog shows, dog-themed events, vets, Crufts and dog charities. You are guaranteed that the visitors to these places - online and off - love dogs, and many of them will be your ideal customer.

I'll use my example:

When I began painting in 2010, I painted ONLY shoes in watercolour and ink. Not another subject did I paint for TWO YEARS! Mostly high-heeled shoes, many of which were designed by the brand Irregular Choice - it was very easy to find my customers - shoe shops, ladies' events, boutiques, Irregular Choice themselves!! I became known in those two years as 'the shoe lady'... I'm still often reminded or contacted about shoe paintings. Can you imagine how much money I've made from shoe paintings, prints, cards, gifts, and calendars over the years? I stopped painting shoes in 2013, yet I still print cards which feature paintings I did 10 years ago... and they still sell!

Now, after the shoes, I started painting vintage items: type-writers, telephones, sewing machines - those grew another group of customers, a new ideal client to add to my shoe buyers.

In 2014, I started painting landscapes, adding a different group of customers again. In 2022, I had my first solo abstract exhibition, and again, I collected more new customers.

As your reputation and your customer base grow, it's less important to be so niche-focused but I still return to 'Who is my ideal client' when I'm marketing a new series of paint-ings or products or a new class or programme. I have an ideal client for each different part of my business.

In the beginning, it's so much easier - you just need to nail your niche, find out everything you need to know about your ideal client and then speak directly to them, using their language - that's your sweet spot.

Honing and focusing on your niche will help you become KNOWN for your work and then customers will come searching for you.

Many artists struggle to find their niche but there are ways to draw it out (see what I did there?).

Style

You may have a very distinct style, and use a certain range of mediums or techniques that you're known for.

Interest

Do you have a hobby or an interest that may tie in with your artwork?

- Gardening,
- Tattoos,
- Kayaking,
- Textiles,
- Horses,
- Shoes ??

I know of an artist locally who goes to every village wedding and paints in the churchyard. How many couples or wedding guests buy that painting, or the prints from it?

Location

Can you focus on creating work featuring your local area or a tourist spot? Featuring the streets, buildings, and landmarks - creating prints and souvenirs to sell.

Mission

Do you support a certain charity? Could your work revolve around that, donating a percentage of the sales?

Of course, it may be coastal painting in the Hebrides, red-roofed cottages in bright landscapes - definitely a much wider niche, but still very targetable.

And remember, ALWAYS paint or create what you love. If you're producing work purely for commercial purposes, both you and your customer will get bored with your work very quickly.

FEEL THE LOVE exercise:

Here are a few questions and journalling prompts that can help nail your niche.

Grab a pen, pour yourself a cup of something lovely and allow these questions to settle in. Allow the answers to come, you might not have all of the answers right now… and yeah, it's all about the love:

- What do I love to paint?
- What mediums and techniques do I love to use?
- What specific things make my art stand out as mine?
- What piece of artwork just flowed effortlessly and why?
- What piece of artwork did I paint purely for me?
- Where is my favourite place in the world?
- Where is my favourite place locally?
- What are my hobbies and interests?

- What causes am I passionate about?

Write down three different niche options you've found from the previous exercise.

Which has the strongest pull for you? Which do you feel is most aligned to the work you produce EASILY in the flow?

11

WHY ARE YOU SO DARNED IRRESISTIBLE?

Finding your ideal customer

Now you've nailed your niche, you've made like Marmite, the next stages in your journey are: firstly, to KNOW who your ideal client is, secondly, to know WHERE they hang out, and thirdly, to know HOW to communicate with them and what language they use.

This body of knowledge will arm you with ALL you need to know about the artwork you make, the products you create, the offers you put out there, the prices you charge, how you sell, where you sell and what experience you must offer!

Reread that paragraph. This is EVERYTHING you need to make a successful business, not just an art business, but ANY business! Powerful stuff.

Go on, reread it just to be sure

If, in the last chapter, Make like Marmite, you doubted your need to niche or just refuse to constrain yourself, then you're going to find this chapter (and creating a successful business) challenging. You'll waste money producing work, products, and offers that you can't sell because you've no idea who they're for. You'll waste time marketing and promoting to anyone who'll listen, whether they like and can afford your work or not. And you'll become frustrated, fed up, and most probably unsuccessful in generating the income or building the business you had hoped for. Why? Because you were adamant that you didn't want or need to find your niche.

If you need to return to the exercises in the last chapter, go now, and join us here when you've Nailed your Niche.

Your IDEAL CLIENT can also be referred to as your TARGET MARKET - it simply means the RIGHT buyer for your products and services. They are someone who:

- Loves your work and connects with you as an artist,
- Usually shares similar values as yourself,
- Appreciates the value in your work, products and offers,
- Can afford your work, services and offers.

I've added a few exercises below to help refine your ideal client avatar. If you're creating work from love, from your passion, it's not uncommon to find that your ideal client is a mirror of yourself. If this is the case - ideal, this allows us to communicate much more easily with them, it allows us to understand what they need and want... and to provide that! Let me know if you find this.

Let's have a closer look at your target market. Use the questions below to draw a clear picture of your ideal customer. If you want to take the questions further, go for it! The more information you have, the better it will serve you going forward.

WHAT DO YOU KNOW ABOUT YOUR IDEAL CUSTOMER:

Write a list of different types or groups of people to whom your niche will appeal.

E.g., I used to paint shoes - so my niche audience might be:

Shoeaholics,

The specific brand of shoe lover (Irregular Choice, for example),

Independent shoe shops,

Women's boutiques,

New mums (baby shoes).

Now take it a stage further.

Choose one type or group and drill down further. Really think about that one person.

Write 10 sentences about your person/group - guess the approximate age, sex, do they have family? Do they work? Income?

WHERE WILL YOU FIND YOUR IDEAL CUSTOMER:

You've investigated who might love your work and you've identified your perfect customer - now the question is:

- WHERE will you find these people?
- WHERE do they hang out online? In 'real life'?

E.g., Do they frequent art groups, exhibitions, Facebook or insta? Galleries? Shoe shops? Coffee shops?

HOW CAN YOU COMMUNICATE WITH YOUR IDEAL CUSTOMER?

- You know who loves your work,
- You know why they love your work,
- You know where you'll find them,

It's time to woo them, court them - allow them to get to know you, like you, trust you.

It's time to start showing up. How will you do this? Write a list of ways to woo, to get in front of your ideal customer, online and off.

E.g., It might be going live on Facebook, if that's where they hang out. It might be a traditional postcard every month, an e-newsletter, it might be a behind-the-scenes insta series, it might be at local fairs, clubs and groups or nationwide events… the list is endless. Be the creative genius you are!

12

____

PICK & MIX

M

ULTIPLE INCOME STREAMS - The WHAT - is my favourite module in DBASA!!

Choosing the right mix of multiple income streams, for me, is like a humungous Woolworths pick & mix of business ideas.

The mix you choose will be very personal to you and your business - your chance to create a giant bag of treats to tempt your ideal customer!

Which will you add?

Which haven't you tried before?

Which makes you sick at the very thought?

Which are your favourites?

Before leaping in and trying everything - cos you'll make yourself sick - I'd like you to think about TWO things:

Two things that will impact which 'sweeties' you choose.

Two things that will help choose the right combination for your business and your customers.

1. Your ASCENSION pyramid

This sounds very grand but it's not.

Think about layers of pricing.

Think about the price you'll charge for your products and offers.

I work on 5 layers or levels of price bands:

FREE - LOW COST - MID COST - HIGH COST - VIP

You may well start with just 3 - low, mid, high - and only you can decide what 'low', 'mid', 'high' means in terms of monetary value.

For example:

LOW - Stationery £2.50 - £10

MID - £50 prints

HIGH - £150 original painting

If you're offering classes, retreats, or online teaching, then these bands will rise according to your prices. No matter what your price is, always aim to have different price bands as:

1. It allows your customer to experience buying from you - starting small to build trust.
2. If a customer can't afford your high offer, they can still enjoy the process of buying from you in a small way.
3. Low offers can be easier to sell, especially if you're still having money mindset issues. You'll sell more of them and therefore create a steady income stream.

2. Different types of business models

Kinda like - don't put your eggs all in one basket!

For consistent sales, consider adding different business models into your mix:

- PRODUCT
- SERVICE
- PASSIVE
- SEMI-PASSIVE
- RECURRING REVENUE

Adding a recurring revenue product will ensure you have good cash flow.

Passive and Semi Passive models will generate income with less effort from you.

Keeping these two things in mind, get your sweetie bag ready as we move on to the good part!!

CHOOSING YOUR SWEETIES!

There are so many ways to make money from your art.

You can't, won't, and shouldn't do it all at once.

Some won't suit your business model at all.

Some will be irrelevant to your business.

There will be some you do NOT want to pursue.

This is what makes you and your business unique.

There is no right or wrong, only your choices based on what YOU like, what investment, if any, you have to make, and what YOUR business can offer.

Original sales:

Selling actual paintings and commissions online or offline, or via Galleries and Exhibitions.

The traditional way to make money as an artist. If selling through galleries or exhibitions, your selling price will be subject to a commission charge - normally 25% - 40%

Print sales:

Paper prints, mounted prints, framed prints, canvas prints, hand-finished prints, limited edition prints, giclee prints.

There are so many ways to sell prints: you can print and hold stock, print to order, drop ship for passive income or use a broker who sells your prints and you'll get a small royalty from sales.

WARNING: if you have a limited edition print - you CANNOT USE THIS IMAGE on ANYTHING ELSE.

Stationery:

First no-brainer - greeting cards. Easy to produce, cheap to produce, no huge stock space needed. Cheap to ship, easy to sell to trade and a great way to market yourself.

Add in notebooks, gift wrap, and calendars for an easy first range.

Product ranges:

It's now so much easier to create product ranges using your images, with many manufacturers online and catering for small businesses who don't want to order massive quantities.

Some are specifically aimed at artists.

Start small, don't get carried away with ordering lots of different products without testing your customer and the sales potential of a few different images and products.

Art materials:

A nice addition if you run classes and can offer materials. Ensure you are paying TRADE/ WHOLESALE prices and making a profit from this - again, start with a small range to find out what your customer needs and wants from you.

Classes and Workshops:

In-person is easier at the beginning to build a reputation and teaching style, which can then be sold online if you choose to do this.

Many artists fear that they're not an 'expert' artist - keep this in mind: you need only KNOW THE MOST IN THAT ROOM AT THAT TIME, so, teaching absolute beginners or children is an easy stepping stone into more advanced classes and workshops.

A good option to start is by being HIRED to teach a class - so you are being paid to deliver a class instead of having to design, sell, and market a workshop on your own.

TIP: DO THE NUMBERS - it's easy to underestimate the cost of venue hire, materials, refreshments AND YOUR TIME.

Online classes:

Can be delivered in 3 ways -

EVERGREEN - DIY pre-recorded with no input from you once filmed.

COMBINATION - pre-recorded with some input from you - perhaps Q&A or live sessions, or a community or group (FB).

LIVE - you deliver all lessons live - this can be stressful as not only are you delivering live, but tech can be problematic at times!

Tuition:

Often the first step into teaching - 121 tuition is very much in demand for people who don't like groups, don't want to attend classes, and don't want to be taught online. The price for private tuition will be much higher as they are getting 100% YOU TIME.

Demos / Talks:

There are so many community groups - from the Women's Institute to art clubs to Rotary clubs - ALL of them searching for speakers and demonstrators!

You won't make a fortune in the smaller circles but once you've done one, you'll get calls to do lots more. I use these to widen my audience. I also take along products to sell on the day - so you can make a few hundred pounds easily in an hour and grow your audience at the same time.

Books / eBooks:

If you have a technique you've honed, why not create an eBook with photos of each step - no cost to create and an excellent passive income stream? Excellent upsell with an evergreen online course.

Retreats / Art Holidays:

Not for everyone - a lot of planning goes into offering a retreat. It can also be very intense and draining if you're running the retreat alone as you need to manage the energy of the group, make sure everyone is happy and also teach.

An option is to collaborate with someone who can take some of that strain and offer another interest in your retreat.

TIP: set the retreat in an area or venue you know

Trade/Wholesale:

Offering your stationery and products to shops and retail is an excellent way to get your name and your work out there.

You'll make much less profit selling to trade but you're selling in large numbers to make up for this - selling to trade is also a very good recurring revenue as retailers need to restock.

Licensing your artwork:

Many card and stationery manufacturers license artwork. Essentially you loan your image to them for a set period - normally 1- 2 years. They can then use it on their products/cards, you'll be credited on reverse. Payment varies but usually, you'll receive a one-off payment and a very low royalty.

WARNING: you CANNOT use this image on ANYTHING during this period!

Homeware and print companies also licence artwork.

Artwork Rental:

It might be originals, it might be prints - new house builders and estate agents all rent artwork to sell houses. Hotels and large commercial premises/offices also rent artwork, usually for an agreed amount of time. Beware of insurance needs - especially if offering original artwork.

Coaching:

If you've done something successfully, and have a track record and a reputation, then perhaps coaching in some aspect of your business might be an option to consider.

Coaching can be very rewarding as you see your student flourish under your guidance.

This list is by no means exhaustive. Thinking laterally and creatively about how and where you can make money doing what you love will make your business stand apart.

Keep an open mind, consider all the options and always keep your eye out for opportunities in unexpected places.

Check out the bonus chapter for 50 more ways to make money as an artist.

13

PRICING FOR PROFIT

One of the questions I'm most asked by students is' how do I price my work?'.

It's kinda like asking 'how long is a bit of string'?

Prints and products, classes and workshops are much easier to price but there are so many different factors to take into consideration when pricing original artwork.

PRICING ORIGINAL ARTWORK

Pricing of original artwork is so ambiguous - it's not a case of simply multiplying the cost of materials by a magic figure, nor allocating an hourly rate to the time taken to create. There is much 'plucking from mid-air', but let's take a look at what factors affect your pricing.

YOU affect your price and YOU are all different - at different stages in your creative journey, with different reputations, using different materials, working in different sizes, framed in different ways, selling in different parts of the world, with different overheads.

The price of your original artwork should take into consideration all of these factors plus more:

How YOU affect the price of your artwork

When someone is buying your work, they're paying for:

- The hours you've taken to learn how to paint/create,
- Your education (art school, college),
- All of the art books you've bought to inspire and educate,
- The workshops/classes you've paid to attend,
- All of the work you've wasted in becoming the artist you are.

How YOUR REPUTATION affects the price

When someone is buying your work, they're paying for YOUR reputation:

- How well-known are you as an artist?
- How many paintings have you sold till now?
- How many paintings have you sold recently?
- Do you have work in exhibitions & galleries?
- Do you have collectors?

How your ARTWORK affects the price

- Medium used,

- Size of the piece,
- Cost of framing/presentation,
- Cost of materials,
- Time taken.

OTHER factors affecting the price

- Where you're selling (commission),
- Charitable percentage or sales (commission),
- Location, location, location,
- How comfortable are you with the price?
- How badly do you want to sell this piece?
- Are you selling to a collector or someone who can improve your artist profile?
- Have you had the painting for a long time?
- Do you want to make quick sales for cash flow?
- Do you just want to sell paintings quickly to improve your profile?
- Is it important that your paintings are accessible to many?

It's not simply the cost of materials plus your hourly rate, plus framing/presentation costs, minus selling fees/commission.

Seriously consider all of the above - and especially the OTHER factors. Some of these are much more personal decisions which will impact your final price.

TIP: If you're unsure, ask your framer for advice. They'll have a very good idea of what's selling at what price in your area.

PRICING PRINTS FOR PROFIT

Prints are much easier to price as they are manufactured and have a production cost. Ideally, you're not directly involved and therefore your time need not be accounted for. You've already done the creative work and it can now become a passive income generator.

I would always advise finding a professional printer to produce and manufacture your prints. Not only will you have a more professional end product, but printing your own costs time, wastage and frustration - you have enough to do without adding these to the equation.

Finding a comparable product is also very easy - the factors affecting the price of your originals have less impact on pricing prints as there will be pricing boundaries (acceptable price range for that exact product in your location).

- Yes, YOU will affect your print RRP, but less so.
- Yes, your REPUTATION will affect your print RRP, but less so.
- Yes, OTHER FACTORS will affect your print RRP, but less so.

Things to keep in mind when pricing prints:

Selling Location - for example, the price of your mounted prints on Etsy will differ from similar mounted prints selling in a gallery in London.

Make sure you use COMPARABLE prints as a guide to your pricing - don't price your standard mounted print in the same way as a museum-quality giclee print. Make sure you check quality and provenance before comparable pricing.

How much your customer is prepared to pay - don't overlook how much your demographic is expecting to pay for your print. Ensure you've researched what your IDEAL customer expects and wants from you before adding any new product to your range.

HAND-FINISHED PRINTS

Hand-finished prints are normally canvas prints with additional work on top. You may just add some brushstrokes in a texture medium to give the look of an original, or you may paint on top of the print, altering the original image.

Either way, a hand-finished print will cost more than a basic print.

Pricing your hand-finished prints should be based upon how 'original' the hand-finishing is - if you've altered the original image by painting on top, then you can most definitely charge more - anything up to 30% of an original at the same size.

However, if you're just adding textural brushstrokes on top of the print, then probably 20% above a standard print price is about right.

PRICING PRODUCTS FOR PROFIT

This is even more simple than pricing prints!

Creating products from your artwork can be a fantastic way to increase your demographic - a potential customer may not want an original, but they DO drink from mugs and use aprons, coasters and phone cases!

A good product range is also a lovely passive or semi-passive income stream. The hard work is done - you need only reorder and sell to benefit from a nice profit margin, so getting the price right is important.

What to think about when pricing your products:

- Cost to manufacture,
- Research comparable products,
- Think about your customer and what they expect to spend,
- Consider where you're selling - on your own or through galleries (commission) or wholesale (trade pricing).

You can work out an acceptable price based on the above.

I will always aim for a minimum of 100% profit on any product. **This does not apply to trade/wholesale**

If I can't get 100% profit, then I need to consider if this product is right for my range or if I'm happy to accept less profit on this product.

PRICING FOR TRADE / WHOLESALE CUSTOMERS

- Selling to trade is all about getting your 'stuff' in front of a massive audience.

- Selling in bulk reduces the price you sell for AND the profit you make.
- Selling to trade means VOLUME.

Retail customers / Trade customers will multiply YOUR trade prices by a minimum of 2.5/3 to reach their retail price.

KEEP THIS IN MIND WHEN PRICING FOR TRADE.

Work back from the retail price of your product to ascertain whether a product will work in your trade range.

REMEMBER, YOU MUST ALSO MAKE A PROFIT!

It is very easy to become a BUSY FOOL, fulfilling lots of orders for very little profit, so getting your pricing right here is imperative if you choose to add Trade customers to your business model.

PRICING CLASSES and WORKSHOPS

The pricing of classes and workshops is more of an arithmetic task due to the costs involved:

- Rent.
- Materials.
- Refreshments.
- Your time.

Add up all of the above

PLUS

what YOU'D like to be paid for hosting the class.

DIVIDE

by the IDEAL NUMBER of workshop attendants.

= Cost per head

Initially, it's worthwhile looking at similar classes and workshops in your area to get an idea of the acceptable selling price.

However, although I will use the formula above as a basis for my class and workshop pricing, my workshop pricing takes into consideration the whole EXPERIENCE I can offer.

What can you add to make your class or workshop different? How can you add value and create an experience for which people are prepared to pay more?

TIP: And this question should apply to everything you do, if you over-deliver, create an extra experience in every aspect of your business - even if it's sending a handwritten card with an online order - this is how you'll build your reputation and stand out in the eyes of your customers, ... ensuring repeat sales and guaranteeing you'll have customers who'll pay for your goods and services.

14

SELLING ONLINE

Selling online has never been easier, nor has it ever been more popular. Conventional sales globally have changed beyond recognition in the past 10 years, especially since the pandemic, as people are becoming much more familiar and trusting with buying online.

And you now have a whole world full of potential customers at your fingertips!

Whether you're drop shipping, posting, supplying and teaching digitally, growing your audience and customer base, or finding your ideal customer, online has never been easier… even the tech has gotten easier, becoming much more user-friendly and intuitive - we can take better pictures, take videos, and talk to customers live - all online. We have hardly any reason to leave the house anymore!!

There are lots of ways to sell online: Existing sites/shops that have already grown a massive audience are just ready, willing and able to buy what you have to offer. Or you could sell directly via your mailing list, your website and your social media accounts.

Each has its limitations, each has costs attached, and each has different levels of involvement and set-up. There is no right or wrong way to sell online, it's about testing to see what works best for you. You can even decide to sell across ALL of these online portals. I'd suggest you DO try a few out to find the right fit.

SELLING VIA EXISTING ONLINE MARKETPLACES

The most common in the UK are Etsy, Shopify, Folksy, and eBay.

These marketplaces are already set up to sell, very simple to use and there's no need to worry about the tech behind it.

Create an account, connect your business bank account to be paid, add your photos of your work or products, set your pricing and postage (if applicable) and publish and wait for the sales to come in (Remember, you must market your new shop). Fulfil the orders by following the steps required and your payment will be sent via the shop to your bank account within a few days.

Then just sit back and wait for lovely feedback from a very happy (possibly repeat) customer.

Pros:

- Everything is already set up, so no tech issues.

- Existing massive audience of potential customers.
- Customers feel safe buying from a recognised shopping platform and will buy more readily.
- Seamless payments direct to your bank.
- Allows you to look professional immediately with no e-commerce outlay.
- It's easy to use from a selling & buying point.
- Can utilise their advertising to attract your ideal customer.

Cons:

- Fees - listing fees and high commission fees.
- Can't brand your shop fully.
- You don't hold the customer information automatically. GDPR means you can't start emailing them without permission.
- Digital products: tutorials, demos, courses - will also have VAT charged on top of all other fees - even if you're not VAT registered.

SELLING VIA YOUR WEBSITE

At some point, you may want to add an e-commerce leg to your website. This means that a 'shopping software' will be added to your site and run similarly to Etsy, etc.

Some sites cannot have this added and you may need to have a new site built specifically to host the e-commerce software.

Pros:

- No extra fees - other than the fee for accepting payments via Stripe or similar and for the software subscription.
- You hold the database for anyone buying, meaning you can market directly to them, making it easier to build relationships.
- Everything will be branded as your business.
- Allows more control over how your shop looks and variations.
- Keeps potential customers on your website - if they find your website, and then find you also sell online, they're more likely to buy.

Cons:

- If tech goes wrong, you (or your tech guy) have to put it right.
- Setting up an e-comm site can be expensive.
- Nobody will know it's there unless YOU tell them. So MUCH more marketing is required needed to direct customers to your shop.
- You'll also pay Stripe or payment software fees and have to set this up along with your e-comm site.

SELLING VIA YOUR MAILING LIST

Your mailing list is a very important part of your business - don't overlook this. Social media accounts do not replace your mailing list!

No matter how many followers you have on social media, you do not own that platform or its contacts so it's supremely important that you start to gather contacts in your mailing list as soon as possible.

Your mailing list can be used for selling, marketing, building relationships etc., accelerating that KNOW, LIKE, TRUST process we talk about.

Selling to your mailing list can take different forms:

It might mean sending a link to your Etsy shop or to your website shop when you've added a new product or have a special offer.

Or it might simply mean sending pictures and info about new products and asking them to get in touch if they are interested in buying!

But you can't do any of these until you have a mailing list.

Which mailing list software should I use?

I would love to be able to advise on which is best BUT it's all down to which you prefer to use.

They all do roughly the same things and most (if not all) offer FREE TRIALS. My best advice is to use these free trials and play around to find out which makes more sense to you.

Some of the most popular are: Mailerlite, Mailchimp, Active Campaign, Constant Contact.

And you should be able to choose a free plan at the beginning, which will allow you to send out newsletters and build your mailing list before delving into customer growth funnels, landing pages etc.

Pros:

- You can be SPECIFIC about your target. Splitting your mailing list into different kinds of buyers (i.e., a list for customers who buy classes and courses, a list for customers who buy paintings, a list for customers who buy kitchenware etc.) will gain more sales as you're not just sending blanket emails to everyone.
- Customers can reply to your email asking questions about your offers, which leads to a more engaged audience (KNOW, LIKE, TRUST) and offers a better, more personal experience.
- More control over what you sell - if you've over-ordered sheep mugs, you can contact your mailing list with a special sheep mug offer!

Cons:

- You have to be consistent.
- If you hate tech, you may get frustrated by having to create digital marketing, newsletters, emails, etc., however, there are loads of people offering this as a business service now so it's relatively easy to outsource.

SELLING VIA ARTIST ON-DEMAND SITES

Usually worldwide sites: Wraptious, Red Bubble, Zazzle, Printful.

If creating products online, taking product shots, or dealing with online selling isn't for you then there are a lot of print-on-demand sites aimed at artists out there.

There are a few in the UK but they are usually based around the globe as the distance is no object, therefore you have a potentially global customer base.

- Upload your artwork to their online portal and see it on the different products they offer.
- They'll then sell on their site to THEIR CUSTOMERS.
- You'll receive a nominal payment for the privilege.

Pros:

- It's easy!
- Your artwork will have the potential to reach a massive audience.

Cons:

- You make very, very little income.
- These are not your customers; they have no idea who you are - you have no idea who they are.
- You have no control over the quality of products - a poor-quality item will reflect badly on your brand.

SELLING VIA YOUR SOCIAL MEDIA ACCOUNTS

This is more about marketing than selling - I would always recommend posting your sales platforms and products on your social media sites.

This is a no-brainer for marketing, but keep in mind:

- Only ONE in every FOUR posts should be selling or your audience will get fed up.
- Make it easy for people to buy by adding the LINK to your post.
- Use the FB and Insta option of a selling button on your pic - easily set up to link to your shop.
- Don't be afraid to DM someone if you think they might like what you have to offer (only 25% of your audience will see all of your posts!!).
- DO NOT SELL on your Personal FB account (you'll get blocked).

THINGS TO REMEMBER FOR ALL ONLINE SELLING PLATFORMS

- Make sure you take GOOD photos.
- Light your product well and take pictures of paintings in bright natural light.
- Take as many pictures as possible of every aspect of your product.
- Give as much information as possible, including sizes.

- Be honest about delivery and lead times –
  remember, under promise/over deliver.
- If a product is a print on demand, explain that fact
  and give an approximate production time.
- WEIGH everything and find accurate postage - DO
  NOT guesstimate postage!
- Follow up with an email, if possible, to ensure all is
  well.
- Pop a business card (or even a greeting card) in with
  the order.

15

SELLING OFFLINE

Isn't it funny how I'm describing this chapter as selling 'offline' - as if online is the norm, even though 'offline', or the traditional ways of selling, existed centuries before the world wide web ever existed? It's a funny old world.

Back to the business at hand!

Selling offline is the traditional route to market for artists and creatives, but it's good to build a portfolio of selling platforms to include both online and off so don't overlook 'old school' selling because there are many valid reasons to get your actual, real life, living, breathing face in front of your customer!

You've heard the adage: People buy from people. Building in-person relationships take a lot of courting, a lot of wooing, and a lot of smiling and chatting.

TIP: Building offline relationships should also be supported by online communication where possible to speed up the relationship building, so keep gathering that all-important email database of customers.

PROS OF SELLING OFFLINE

There are TWO big positives to selling offline, looking your customer in the eye:

1. Accelerating the KNOW, LIKE, TRUST process

- It's much easier to build relationships face-to-face.
- Much quicker to build a rapport with your customer.
- Much quicker to accelerate through KNOW, LIKE, TRUST…
- and therefore, quicker to convert a potential customer to a buyer.

2. Feedback

- You have no idea how valuable seeing, first-hand, the response to your work, products, and services, offers is.
- To have the opportunity to ASK your customer what they like, dislike, what they would like to see etc., is absolute GOLD!
- Your customer will feel loved and valued when you ask their opinion (again, accelerating the KNOW, LIKE, TRUST).

- You'll gain FREE product development feedback and information, allowing you to create exactly what your customer wants to buy.
- Minimising risk, minimising costs in creating new products, work and offers.

SELLING VIA GALLERIES

Often the very first route to market and is most traditionally associated with an artist selling their work.

Pros:

- The gallery already has a customer base - they'll have a market for your work already.
- They'll advertise or market your work, giving you access to a bigger audience and allowing people to see your work who are not in your marketing circle.
- You can add the gallery to your CV, adding to your reputation as an artist.

Cons:

- Customers belong to the GALLERY; these are not your customers - ordinarily, after a sale, you won't know who has bought your work unless the buyer contacts you directly.
- COMMISSION – The gallery will take a commission from your work ranging from 25% - 40%.
- PAYMENT – It can take a while to get payment - 30-60 days post-sale is standard.

- You have no control over where or how your work is displayed. The gallery may choose to remove your work without notice.
- If the gallery is also a framer, they may insist that they frame your work

TIP: Choose carefully - research thoroughly.

- Before approaching a gallery, RESEARCH the work they already sell.
- Choose a gallery that sells work similar in style and subject matter to your own. If a gallery sells lots of wildlife paintings, they're unlikely to want big bright abstracts because they know their customers and they know what sells for them: wildlife paintings.

SELLING VIA EXHIBITIONS

It is ALWAYS worth entering exhibitions - Keep an eye out for any local exhibitions to get started.

PROS:

- They usually take less commission - approximately 25% is standard for exhibitions unless it's a charity exhibition, then it's likely to sit at 50%.
- It gives you access to a wider audience if it's a group exhibition.
- There's a chance to be 'spotted' by a gallery or a collector.

There are no CONS in entering exhibitions - a hanging fee is normal but doesn't pay over the odds.

TIP:

- *Ensure you follow their hanging guidelines (hooks, etc.).*
- *Have your work framed professionally.*

SELLING VIA LOCAL SHOPS / CAFES

If you're in a small town/village, an easy first step is to offer your work and products to a local shop, cafe, or garden centre.

This will normally be on a SALE OR RETURN basis, e.g., the shop will take a commission for any sales but won't pay you upfront.

TIP:

- *Negotiate a commission rate you're comfortable with and specify YOUR prices AND confirm when you'll be paid for any sales.*
- *Supply an artist bio for customers to read about you and have business cards to take away so customers can contact you directly.*
- *Do NOT leave your work for months if it's not selling - it does you NO favours.*

SELLING VIA OPEN STUDIO AND COLLABORATIONS

Popping up all over the place, Open Studios have become big over the past 10 years.

Open Studios kicked off as exactly that - an artist opened their studio inviting customers to visit, to see behind the scenes and see their work processes. This was actually really interesting - nothing better than a good rummage in someone else's studio, finding out how they work!

However, over the past few years, it's changed a bit - many artists don't have spaces to visit or don't want people visiting their homes, so they are often now hosted in larger venues where artists can set up their 'show' – which, in turn, brings bigger numbers of visitors (one stone, many birds concept).

I'd encourage anyone starting off to get involved with their local Open Studios - they're well marketed, well attended, you'll have the support of other creatives, and you're able to gather info for your mailing list (with a simple form to fill in), and NO COMMISSION is charged on any sales.

Another great situation is to get feedback from potential customers and the perfect opportunity to take experimental work, unframed work, sketchbooks etc. Expect to pay a joining fee, but you'll get loads of marketing.

SELLING VIA EVENTS, MARKETS & FAIRS

This is where you'll get the BEST feedback for your work and products.

The cost of buying a table or stand at a fair varies MASSIVELY - ranging from local craft fairs, school fairs, and village fetes - right up to national fairs and events like Country Living.

Expect to pay £10-£25 for a local stand for the day and approximately £400 per sq metre in a 4-day national fair.

Keep in mind you also need to buy stock to sell - this is included in your costs before you can start to make a profit.

TIP:

- **Research the big fairs thoroughly - their sales team will sell their granny to fill a stand!**
- **Look at your Ideal Client description - do your ideal customers hang out here?**

SMALL LOCAL FAIRS - Pros

- Low cost;
- Gives you exposure to a local demographic;
- Great feedback opportunity;
- Often supporting a local charity, so it's an opportunity to shout about that in Socials.

Cons

- Can be a lot of work for not a lot of profit;

- Unlikely to have your ideal client - mixed demographic;
- Can be soul-destroying if footfall and response are poor.

NATIONAL FAIRS - Pros

- Massive footfall/opportunity to massively grow your audience and gain new customers;
- If you've done your research, it should offer a high percentage of your Ideal Client;
- National fairs will market their event very well, hijack that and use it for your audience growth.

Cons

- BIG COST - in the stand, stock, travel and accommodation - therefore high risk;
- TIRING - usually, 4 days, plus one day set up, plus any travel time;
- Don't underestimate build-up, breakdown and weeks to prep.

SELLING VIA TRADE / WHOLESALE

This is a different beast - you're selling to shops and retail outlets who will then add on their margin and sell your work/products to THEIR customers.

Selling to Trade at wholesale pricing is a simpler way to nab yourself a bigger audience.

However, in return for someone else (shop) doing all the selling, promoting, and marketing, you'll make much less profit.

Trade pricing is different.

Your trade customer will multiply YOUR trade price by a minimum of 2.5.

Keep this in mind when pricing - for the trade customer, it's ALL about the price.

e.g., Greeting card sells at £2.50 - Your price to trade/wholesale is £1.

To reach trade customers, your easiest way is to book a stand at a TRADE FAIR, allowing you to connect with lots of engaged buyers. Trade fairs are national fairs (between 2-5 days) and usually twice annually: Spring (Jan) and Autumn (Sept).

Only shop owners / retail buyers attend to buy new stock for their outlets.

These are much more business-like events - but don't underestimate the need for courting - this is still people buying from people. They are just buying commercially, not buying from their heart - always thinking about THEIR profit and THEIR customers.

They're interested in:

profit margins / best-selling designs / shipping costs / delivery times / payment terms minimum order quantities (you'll sell bulk quantities, not single items).

Pros:

- Allows you to reach many more people and cover a much bigger geographical area;
- Great for the CV to add a list of stockists;
- Gets your work out there - make sure all your details are on the reverse of cards, calendars etc., so new customers can reach you directly;
- Once the relationship has been formed, re-orders give a very steady income.

Cons:

- Much less profit for you;
- If you're not a fan of packing, posting etc., this can be tedious!
- If it starts to impact your business, I'd recommend order packing only once per week (remember to manage customer expectations), using a fulfilment centre for cards, or employing someone casually to pack orders for you;
- Setting up the brochures, pricing, invoicing and keeping control of your stock can be time-consuming - but necessary - however, this can be done by a part-time admin assistant or freelancer if it becomes too much.

TIP:

- ***Start with a tight range of products!***
- ***Make buying from you simple with order forms, a simple brochure, and price lists.***
- ***Manage their expectations - don't say you'll deliver quickly if you can't. It's best to under promise, over deliver - if you do it right, you'll have re-orders, which is the name of the game in this one.***
- ***Keep in touch with your trade customers, and ask if they need top-ups - they often don't have time and the person who DOES get in touch will get the business.***

16

BRANDING AND MARKETING, MARKETING AND BRANDING

'm just going to touch lightly on this subject here as this is a much more interactive subject which I LOVE to teach live, allowing me to compare examples and illustrate how simple branding and marketing can be.

If you decide to join my DON'T BE A STARVING ARTIST® live programme, this is one of the longest live sessions I'll host. Being a graphic designer in my previous life, I can forget how much I love the jigsaw that is marketing and branding until this module!

Firstly - Marketing and Branding are bed partners.

Secondly - people make them more complicated than they need to be!

It's all about common sense, keeping it simple, consistency and ALWAYS, ALWAYS keeping in mind your ideal customer.

This pair work hand-in-hand to create an image and the voice of your company, products and services that become familiar to your customers.

Marketing and branding are instrumental in getting your customers onto that KNOW, LIKE, TRUST ladder.

BRANDING

A brand is NOT just a logo.

Branding is the process of creating an identity for a company in the mind of a consumer. Branding is made up of a company's logo, visual design, mission, and tone of voice.

Your brand is everything about you and your business - from your logo, the fonts you use, colour palettes, how you communicate in person and online, the language you use and the tone of your communication, the design of your marketing materials, how you package orders, what experience you offer on top of every sale.

YOU are your brand; your brand is YOU.

Do not overcomplicate your needs when creating your brand elements - create a simple style to use for every online or print communication.

Graphic design used to be a costly process if you wanted a quality product, hey, it still is! Having worked as a graphic designer for over 20 years, I know how expensive it can be.

THE GOOD NEWS IS there are now lots of fantastic online platforms which negate the need in employing a designer or buying expensive software like Photoshop or illustrator. My favourite is Canva but check them out and see what feels best for you.

AN EASY WAY TO CREATE YOUR BRANDING STYLE OR BRAND GUIDELINES

- Choose FIVE colours that all work well together - use ONLY these in all communications.
- Choose TWO fonts - one with a bit of flourish and one sans serif (no flicky bits).
- Photography - what style of photos will you use? Check out lifestyle and brand photography on Pinterest for ideas.
- Logo - create a simple logo (less is more) - ensure you use the colours & fonts above - it may well just be your name, and that's ok!
- How will you choose to speak? Formal? Casual? Fun?

MARKETING

Marketing is the practice of increasing awareness, consideration, purchase/repurchase and preference for a product or service through consumer-driven benefits, advertising, packaging, placement, pricing and promotions.

A marketing plan is simply a plan of HOW, WHERE and WHAT you'll COMMUNICATE with your customers.

Planning how to market yourself, your business and your products/offers is important - it helps to sell and build trust if done consistently.

CREATING YOUR MARKETING PLAN / STRATEGY

What to consider when planning how you'll market your company, products/services:

YOUR IDEAL CUSTOMER IS KEY

Where do they hang out:

Where online? Which groups are they part of? What magazines or newspapers do they read?

There is no point in paying for magazine advertising if your customer is under 25 and hangs out in Tik Tok, however, if you paint farm animals - especially people with special breeds - then perhaps it's worth investigating advertorials or advertising in Farming Weekly.

If you want to increase your reach in another area, then investigate online groups and publications.

If your customer actively takes part in local groups, get in touch - can you do a demo or speak at a group meeting?

These are all things to think about when considering where and how to speak to your customers - again, these are all just questions surrounding YOUR IDEAL CUSTOMER.

DIFFERENT WAYS TO MARKET

There are sooooo many ways to market yourself and this list is just a tiny drop in the ocean:

FREE

Social media; demos; doing lives; talking in other groups online & off; emailing your database; competitions (only paying for the prize); podcasts; interviews.

PAID

Traditional advertising in newspapers/magazines; online advertising; flyers; door drops; leaflets; website; sponsoring opportunities.

Be creative - that's what you're best at. Take your customers by surprise, pop up when least expected, you'll stand out from the crowd if you do things differently.

17

PLANNING

S o here we are, in our final chapter, and I'd like to thank you for hanging on in there because I know, as a fellow non-finisher, reading to the end of a book can be a hard slog!

I do hope you've been inspired and you've enjoyed reading about how to make money as an artist but most of all, I hope you are bursting with ideas and ready to get started! Now is the time to start planning your creative future, planning to live life in colour.

How big is your appetite? What multiple income streams will you add to your 'sweetie bag'?

Head back to the big Woollies pick 'n' mix of business ideas and try a few that you like the look of. There's no need to overindulge, don't make yourself sick. You'll also find 50 more ways to make money from your work in the next bonus chapter!

The choices you make will be led by the time you have to spend, and the money (if any) you have to spend... you can create a profitable art business without spending a bean by choosing drop shipping, online teaching, and selling originals unframed and unmounted.

Remember to think about adding DIFFERENT PRICE POINTS to your products, offers and services - offering an entry-level purchase can be the start of a lucrative customer relationship that, over time, grows in value to your business.

You are in control of how much you add and what elements you'd like to add. Focus only on your path - 'Stay in your Lane' is a great phrase to remind yourself not to be distracted by what others are doing. This is YOUR business; this is your chance to craft something that makes your heart sing... and makes you money!

Grab yourself a calendar or planner - I print off A4 calendar sheets and use a pencil before committing to fixed dates. Plan where you might launch your products, when you might sell, when you'll market your offers, and how you'll communicate with and grow your audience. Start your notebook of ideas and journalling to strengthen your artist mindset.

REMEMBER:

Your IDEAL CUSTOMER - do the work, really find out who he/she is, what they like, what they want from you, how they like to buy, where they like to buy and what they're willing to pay.

REMEMBER:

To PRICE FOR PROFIT - do not be a busy fool, this IS a business.

REMEMBER:

To consider ways to make money PASSIVELY, SEMI PASSIVELY and RECURRING.

REMEMBER:

PEOPLE BUY FROM PEOPLE - be honest, be genuine, be upfront and be yourself.

And always remember…

You ARE an artist and you CAN make money doing what you love!

BONUS CHAPTER

50 OTHER ways to make money creatively without selling
your art.

This book contains only a fragment of ways to make money as an artist - opportunities can exist in the most unlikely places. Think laterally and creatively. Here are a few more to add to your sweetie bag:

1. Publish a book on your story (come on, I've got to get this in first!) - how you became an artist, how you create, and what techniques you use. It could be a visual book, with step-by-step pictures.
2. Host your paint parties - sip and paint, slurps and turps - perfect for groups of friends and families. Could be themed for special events like hen parties, baby showers, or Christmas.
3. Create a local landmark range of souvenirs from your artwork to sell yourself or in gift shops and

retail outlets locally. Stickers, bookmarks, notebooks, mini canvas prints, etc.

4. Organize creative wellness retreats - partner up with teachers of yoga, pilates, and meditation - find a caterer or a facility that makes delicious wholesome food and create a restorative creative retreat.
5. Paint wedding bouquet commissions - perfect wedding gift for the bride.
6. Paint teddy/cuddly toy commissions - perfect baby gift.
7. Start an art rental business for local hotels, guest houses, Airbnb, rented accommodation, offices and public spaces.
8. Become a mural painter.
9. Offer critiques and feedback to emerging artists or students' portfolios for art school application.
10. Become an illustrator - illustrate your own book!
11. Paint ONTO clothes, bags, shoes etc., and create a range of wearable artwork.
12. Paint pet portraits at pet rescue centres - offer charitable donations with every sale, and create a set of greeting cards for the centre to use.
13. Design branded social media posts for non-tech artists.
14. Pimp and upcycle picture frames and sell to other artists or use them on your work to stand out.
15. Host live or online painting sessions - a regular group opportunity to come together, enjoy the support and discuss your work - like a Stitch & Bitch session.

16. Start after-school art/craft classes - there's a massive demand for this.

17. Offer to run simple, short, art classes to care homes for the elderly.

18. Paint at live events - weddings, theatre, corporate days etc. Take pre-orders for prints post event and/or auction/sell your originals.

19. Create a monthly online programme for primary school teachers, offering complete art lesson plans for their students.

20. Start an Open Studio event in your area if none exists already - or collaborate with another couple of artists and host your own.

21. Become a curator for small galleries - offering curation and hanging services for new exhibitions.

22. Host Plein air workshops locally - find the best spots to paint, offer a complete guide on how to set up when painting outdoors and how to find the best composition, etc. Remember to have a Plan B if your weather is likely to be inclement.

23. Open an Artist Co-op Space - rent an unused shop, building, or garage and rent space to other artists - plan mini-exhibitions, studio nights & classes as a collective.

24. Coach artists through their first exhibition - framing/presentation advice, marketing, pricing, planning and curation.

25. Alternative paint maker - using alternative raw materials, run workshops on how to create paint from natural sources. NEVER buy a tube of pre-mixed green again!

26. Paper maker - if you love making your own paper, teach artists how to create their own surfaces.

27. Journal/sketchbook maker - using your own papers, old maps, and letters - teach how to assimilate surfaces and build your own sketchbook.

28. Host a nature retreat - foraging for materials to use in your artwork, papers and as drawing/painting materials - mixed media, sculpture, photography. Throw in a campfire and some glamping for a bigger experience.

29. Host a coastal retreat - seagrass and driftwood make fabulous sculptures, pieces of jewellery, or can be used to create mixed media artworks.

30. Record guided visualisations for artists to encourage creativity or move beyond artist block.

31. Teach how to create a travel sketchbook/journal - what to collect while travelling, the perfect travel art kit, quick tips & techniques to use while there (you'll find this very course in www.artacademy.uk - one of my favourites!)

32. Offer a print-on-demand design service to other less tech-savvy artists so they can have their range of products without the pain of having to learn the tech.

33. Create an art material review blog - test art products and materials offering reviews and offer affiliate links through the retailer or Amazon - get paid for every product bought.

34. Sell bridal or baby shower painting kits - pre-printed paint by numbers with materials and a step-by-step

video - or run them live, in-person, throw in some fizz and games for a complete experience package.

35. Become an in-house artist for a public venue, offering classes in the space or painting live - consider public conservatories, grand town halls, libraries, stately homes, museums, and country gardens.

36. Create a pack of printed collage materials, using your work, to sell to crafters and card makers.

37. Open a local centre or a series of art workshops, employing other artists to deliver a range of different classes and talks.

38. Become a muralist - perfect if you've always wanted to paint big but don't have the space!

39. Host team-building events for corporates - work together to create a piece of artwork that they can hang in their office.

40. Teach specialist hobby groups how to paint their favourite subject - train spotters, bird watchers, horticulturists, specialist animal breeders, dog lovers, kayakers… the list is endless.

41. Develop an art subscription box - monthly, quarterly, annually. Include materials, books, inspiration, lovely things to nibble on, stationery, with a link to a video of a painting demo or talk or reviews.

42. Develop an art subscription box for kids - materials, books, nibbly things and a printed step-by-step guide to painting or creating something.

43. Host an art road trip - plan an interesting route where you can stop to sketch, paint, eat, and stay - think Thelma & Louise without going off the cliff!

44. Coach other artists on how to find their style (or buy my workbook, How to Find your Style in 8 Steps!)

45. Write copy for other artists' websites, PR, and marketing - it's always much, much easier to sell for someone else.

46. Offer to set up other creatives' mailing lists, landing pages, and automated emails - there are so many people out there who have no clue and no interest in this. If you kinda like the tech, get your services out there!

47. Photograph artwork service - taking decent photos of their work is a massive challenge for many artists and the key to producing quality prints and products.

48. Plan an art workshop tour - book & sell art workshops in towns, areas you love or have always wanted to visit.

49. Host a giant paint party to support a local charity - ending with an exhibition or auction of work, donating to the charity.

50. Become a speaker - supporting, inspiring and encouraging other artists to live life in colour, reprogram their minds and take steps NOW to make their dreams of becoming an artist and making money doing what they love a reality.

WAYS TO WORK WITH ME IF YOU'RE A STARVING ARTIST

If you've enjoyed this bite-size version of Don't be a Starving Artist®, if you've been inspired by my story and would love to work through the DBASA® programme, there are a couple of ways you can do this:

DIY Don't be a Starving Artist® Programme

- 12 x modules of pre-recorded learning with accompanying downloadable workbooks;
- Private Facebook community for support, ask any questions you have;
- Lifetime access to all content;
- Work through at your own pace.

https://www.artacademy.uk/courses/DBASA-DIY

LIVE Don't be a Starving Artist® Programme

6-month live programme

Live programme runs annually. kicking off each September

- 12 x weekly modules of pre-recorded learning with accompanying downloadable workbooks;
- 12 x weekly LIVE Q&A sessions;
- 3 x LIVE guest expert sessions;
- 3 x months of Facebook support with monthly LIVE Q&A and monthly LIVE Guest Expert (post programme);
- Private Facebook community for support;
- Lifetime access to all content.

https://www.subscribepage.com/dbasa-waitlist

Bespoke one-to-one Creative Coaching

If you'd like to work with me on a one-to-one basis, your coaching programme will be tailored specifically to your needs. This might be for you if:

- You don't like group programmes;
- You'd like more help in crafting your perfect business;
- You want to get started and selling as quickly as possible;
- You want to access my black book of contacts and suppliers, saving time and money.

I only have limited availability for one-to-one coaching so please drop me a message and we'll have a chat to see if we're a fit and if this is right for you. Email me at gillian@gillianpark.co.uk

KEYNOTE SPEAKER

If you have an audience or event, I'd love to talk about the value of creativity and why we need to harness our creative superpowers, my keynotes are below but can be adapted to your audience.

- The Value of Creativity
- Don't be a Starving Artist
- How to monetise your hobby

CORPORATE CREATIVE WORKSHOPS

I'd love to work with businesses who recognise the value of creativity, who value the mental wellbeing of their workforce and who are interested in exploring how to do things differently, from problem solving to generating new ideas … and who are looking for more than the same old team building workshops!

FREE RESOURCES

FREE FACEBOOK GROUPS

FREE Art Academy Common Room

If you love art, even if you're a total newbie, you'll find loads of inspiration and support here:

https://www.facebook.com/groups/
theartacademycommonroom

FREE Don't be a Starving Artist group

If you're interested in making money doing what you love:

https://www.facebook.com/groups/dbasa

FREE DOWNLOADS

YOU WANNA BE FAST & LOOSE?

How to loosen up your painting and become a more expressive artist

https://www.subscribepage.com/so-you-wanna-be-fast-loose

10 WAYS TO MAKE MONEY FROM 1 PAINTING

https://www.subscribepage.com/10-ways-to-make-money-from-1-painting

ONLINE TEACHING

THE ART ACADEMY - online teaching platform

Lots of different levels of classes, courses & programmes - plus FREE demos and videos:

https://www.artacademy.uk/

MAILING LISTS

WORKSHOPS AND CLASSES

Drop your details here if you'd like more info on new, in-person classes, workshops and retreats:

https://www.subscribepage.com/inpersonworkshops

DON'T TAKE MY WORD FOR IT

Here's what a few students have had to say about Creative Foundations and the Don't be a Starving Artist® Programme.

I began painting during the pandemic and loved it! I wanted to learn more and joined the Art Academy, enrolling in a few different classes.

Little did I know that this would change my life path forever! Gillian's down-to-earth, straight-talking manner resonated with me, and my love for art and developing my own skills grew.

I enrolled on the Creative Foundations Course. Its revelations to me personally were phenomenal and started my journey investigating how I could develop further and actually make money from my art, which

I'd never considered. The natural progression was to sign up to the DBASA® programme. Gillian's leadership skills and informative sessions have proved priceless, her style of delivering is totally unique and yet motivational, and has totally helped me define my future.

Fast forward a few months, and I am now engaging with Gillian on a one-to-one basis. I am now an artist, planning to give up my full-time day job to run my own business. If anyone had said that this would be my journey a couple of years ago, I would have thought they were crazy.

I will always be indebted to Gillian for her guidance and encouragement. My challenge is now to take all that I have learnt and make my business a successful one.

CHRISTINE

With the Creative Foundations course, Gillian challenges you to see yourself as an artist and explore the specifics of your mindset that holds you back from embracing your creative self, and with her wealth of knowledge as a successful artist and businesswoman, she takes you on a journey to really dig into what your own art means to you, in both your style and the business of your audience, whether you have one currently or have a desire to create one and make money from your creativity.

The combination of Gillian's energy, knowledge, and unique style of encouragement, all wrapped up in GP humour, means you want to come back for more.

Gillian is considerate and understanding of where you are on your art or creative journey, being kind and supportive as you need it, whilst at the same time, she can give you real prod when you need it (thanks Gillian). Not forgetting, of course, her wide range of artistic talents and wealth of knowledge as a successful artist.

The Creative Foundations really enables you to create a foundation on which to build as an earning artist or creative.

JILL

"Gillian's Programme was inspirational. It helped focus my thinking and really supported my development. Above all else, it was working together with similar-minded artists, led so skillfully by Gillian, that made it for me.

A great learning experience with lovely people and Gillian just has this amazing ability to get the best out of everyone.

It was never my goal to sell, but much to my surprise and delight, I sold work at the end of the programme and have done since. I've created my own range of cards and prints; I've had a few commissions and I now create and sell work in aid of my favourite charity!"

ELIZABETH

And some feedback from audience members at a recent speaking engagement:

You know you've heard a great talk when you are still speaking about it days later. Not only did Gillian light up the stage with her energy and humour, but she left a mark that has allowed me to embrace my stifled creativity and encourage my clients to do the same.

KIM RAINE: ADHD MIND, BODY AND
CONFIDENCE COACH

Only Gillian could have opened the day, capturing us all in such a way, with her fiery energy, her hilarious sense of humour and of course, her real passion for the power of creativity.

Thanks to a marvellous, eclectic mix of crochet squares, Tony Hart, mindful colouring books and not forgetting the fabulous shoes, we were all left with huge grins on our faces, feeling warm and inspired and thoroughly convinced of the desperate need our world has today for us all to invite more creativity into our lives.

LUCY RENNIE: LR COMMS

My first experience of Gillian Park was when she arrived in all of her effervescent glory on the stage at The Theatre of Dreams, Old Trafford.

She spoke with passion, confidence and humour about a subject that was thought-provoking and extremely important. She was warm and engaging yet delivered her message packed with a colourful punch.

I shall never colour between the lines ever again!

Thank you for bringing energy and joy to the stage. It was an honour to be in your audience.

JULES KELLY: HOLISTIC
TRANSFORMATION & SUCCESS COACH
SPACE & FREEDOM

ABOUT THE AUTHOR

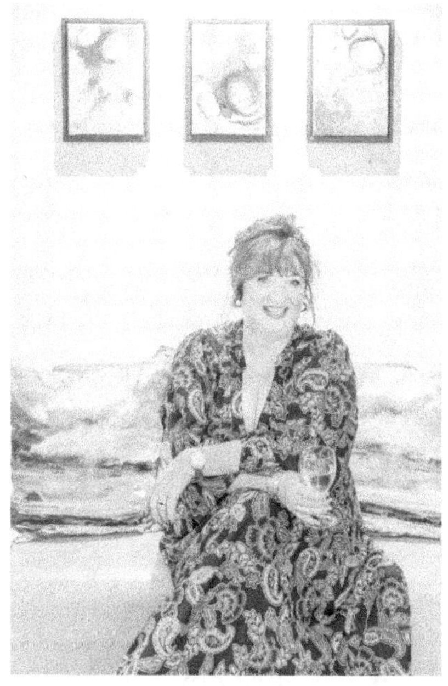

Photo credit: Opening night at Driven to
Abstraction exhibition 2022 Gerri Campbell

Gillian is a professional artist, a multi-award-winning art educator, a public speaker and a creative coach. She actively encourages creativity in everyone, from absolute beginners to professionals, while also coaching artists on how to make money doing what they love.

As a Glasgow School of Art graduate, Gillian enjoyed a career as an award-winning magazine designer before realising, 13 jobs later, that she was wholly unemployable. Chucking the day job in 2004, she launched her own design business specialising in packaging.

Gillian became a full-time professional artist in 2016 and now shares her stable studio with three guinea pigs, surrounded by glorious Ayrshire countryside, and lives next door with her hubby, two daughters and two dogs.

Inspired by her surroundings, Gillian loves to paint big, bold, colourful expressive landscapes and abstracts in oils & pastels and opened her onsite gallery in 2018, where her work is displayed. She exhibits throughout the UK with collectors in Australia, the USA, New Zealand, Hungary, and France and also has a painting in HM King Charles' collection at Dumfries House. Her online Art Academy opened in September 2021 and she has since taught students online as far-flung as North Carolina!

Gillian has a serious shoe fixation, buys hugely unnecessary vintage 'stuff', enjoys a glass or two of wine, loves boxing and crocheting giant, very brightly coloured blankets - but not all at the same time.

Her mission in life is to pioneer the joy of creativity in all, to become the positive artist role model missing in so many young lives, and prove to the world that art IS a real job and you CAN make money doing what you love!

www.gillianpark.co.uk

CONNECT WITH ME

facebook.com/gillianparkartpage

instagram.com/gillianparkart

linkedin.com/in/gillian-park-63427617